DOC!

The Adventures of a Navy Hospital Corpsman

HUGH SULLIVAN

HELLGATE PRESS   ASHLAND, OREGON

DOC!

©2014 Hugh Sullivan

Published by Hellgate Press

(An imprint of L&R Publishing, LLC)

Hellgate Press
PO Box 3531
Ashland, OR 97520
email: info@hellgatepress.com

Editor: Harley B. Patrick
Cover Design: L. Redding

Library of Congress Cataloging-in-Publication Data

Sullivan, Hugh C, Jr., 1942-
  Doc! : the adventures of a Navy corpsman / Hugh Sullivan.
    pages cm.
  ISBN 978-1-55571-772-8
1. Sullivan, Hugh C, Jr., 1942- 2. United States. Navy--Hospital corpsmen--Biography. 3. United States. Navy--Officers--Biography. 4. United States. Navy. Hospital Corps--Biography. 5. Persian Gulf War, 1991--Medical care--United States. 6. Vietnam War, 1961-1975--Medical care--United States. 7. United States. Marine Corps. Marine Regiment, 9th. Battalion, 1st--Biography. 8. Vietnam War, 1961-1975--Personal narratives, American. 9. Persian Gulf War, 1991--Personal narratives, American. I. Title. II. Title: Adventures of a Navy corpsman.
  V63.S84A3 2014
  359.0092--dc23
  [B]
                        2014025454

Printed and bound in the United States of America
First edition 10 9 8 7 6 5 4 3 2 1

This book is dedicated to Wanda—my loving, supportive, and loyal wife of forty-three years.. It was easy at times when I was in the middle of an adventure to forget that Wanda was at home handling everything involving three children—their health, school, and social problems. She took care of all the household matters, including the finances, dealing with broken down cars, plumbing and electrical troubles, and so on, while at the same time holding down a full-time job. There is no way I could ever express my appreciation for what she did to keep our family on firm ground and support my career. And without her prompting I would never have undertaken this book project. Thanks, Wanda, I love you.

AUTHOR'S NOTE

There are instances in telling this story where I do not fully recall all the issues and details, and have taken the liberty to ad-lib a bit in order to keep the story moving. In addition, anyone who knows me and reads this book might be able to identify their aliases. It is my sincere hope that I have not offended any of you and if I have, I apologize.

ONE

YOU COULD SEE THE HEAT WAVES SLIGHTLY ABOVE the asphalt quarter-mile track that surrounded the football field.

"Damn it's hot to be so early in June," Bruce said.

I asked, "Do you think it will be this hot at Great Lakes?"

Bruce laughed and said, "They're probably still digging out from last winter's snow."

"Is there supposed to be some kind of magic about this graduation ceremony tonight that requires two rehearsals before the actual ceremony?"

****

Columbia, South Carolina's (S.C.) Olympia High School Class of 1961 was preparing for graduation on June 2nd. It was the largest graduating class in the history of the school—fifty-two students. Twenty-eight of the graduates started in the first grade together. The entire school from first through twelfth only numbered around 500 students. The school supported the families that primarily worked in the local cotton mills. While this class had its share of honor students, including one headed for the Air Force Academy, it will probably be remembered best for its athletic prowess. This graduating class won two state championships in basketball, two in baseball, and finished the football season that year with a nine and three record, the best in the previous four years. A number of the graduates already had wedding plans, though many joked that dating someone from Olympia was like "dating one's sister or brother."

I made my decision to escape the cotton mill way of life and join the Navy. I signed the necessary papers the Friday before graduation. I was to report to the Federal Courthouse on Monday morning to be part of a recruiting class that was being sent to the Great Lakes Illinois Recruit Training Center for twelve weeks of basic recruit training.

The decision to join the Navy was not a spur of the minute one. It was made three years earlier when I and three older friends decided to borrow (steal) a car to go for a joy ride. It did not take long to find a 1952 Ford with the keys in it. Once we were in the car and out of the general area, the decision was made to go to New York where we would be put up at one of the older guy's cousin's house until we could find jobs.

Unfortunately we had little money, and half a tank of gas would not get us to New York. We were caught by the local police stealing gas from an automobile in South Hill, Virginia. As it turned out this was a Federal offense since we had crossed state lines. I was fifteen at the time and was in a position to have my trial separated from the older boys who were seventeen.

I remained loyal to my friends and refused to rat them out by saying I did not know what was going on. Consequently I was sentenced to five years federal probation. After a couple years of reporting monthly to my probation officer I asked if this would keep me from joining the military. My probation officer indicated that he could get my probation rescinded if I would join the South Carolina National Guard. I joined the following week, just before the beginning of my junior year summer vacation. Good to his word, my probation officer was able to get the remainder of my probation canceled. That summer I spent four weeks at Fort Jackson, South Carolina, undergoing training and digging a lot of foxholes.

I knew I was facing a two-year enlistment as soon as I graduated from high school. My entire senior year I worried about those two years of living in the mud and eating military food that came from WWII warehouses. In May of 1961 I made the decision to talk to the Navy recruiter and see if I could join. Even with the federal probation in my background the Navy accepted me.

I came from a poor but proud family. I got one new pair of shoes at the beginning of school every year and when they wore out I went barefoot. Olympia High School was fairly lax on things like bare feet and even smoking. The kids could smoke anywhere on the grounds of the school except in the classrooms.

My family was not much different than most in the neighborhood. My dad drank too much, but he never got violent when he was drunk. He worked as a welder in the local granite quarry and my mom worked in one of the cotton mills. She worked the third shift, which was from 11:00 p.m. until 7:00 a.m. Both my parents were smokers so I took up smoking at the ripe old age of twelve. Their respective jobs were hard and grueling. While my dad was at work during the day my mom was sleeping. This gave me ample opportunity to get in trouble. While everyone in the community knew one another they were quick to report misbehavior by any of the kids in the neighborhood. My biggest problem seemed to be that I could not avoid fights. I rarely won but would not back down. This attitude probably reduced the number of fights I was actually engaged in. While not a star by any means, I did letter in football and track.

I guess all in all I was lucky to be getting the opportunity to break the chains of the cotton mills.

The graduation was kind of anticlimactic. The biggest event of the ceremony was when three guys who had been drinking since the last rehearsal fell off of the top step of the bleachers and disrupted the ceremony long enough for them to be escorted off stage. The audience was assured that all were ok, that they were just being checked out to make sure they had not broken anything and that they would receive their diplomas after the ceremony.

TWO

TUESDAY, JUNE 5, 1961, I WAS SWORN INTO THE U.S. Navy along with fourteen other guys from the Columbia, S.C. area. We were given a bus ride to the Columbia Regional Airport and from there we flew into Chicago, Illinois.

It did not take long for this adventure to get interesting. When I arrived in Chicago I found that there were about sixty other recruits from around the southeast waiting for transportation to the Recruit Training Center (RTC). All were loaded onto Greyhound busses for the trip. My group of about twenty was anything but quiet and cooperative. One of them found that if you hit the bus window at the top it would fall out. It was built that way for safety reasons. The first time this occurred, the bus driver stopped the bus and gave a stern warning against any further such behavior. He went outside and closed the window. Well what was one to expect?

No sooner was the bus on the road when almost every window on the bus was knocked out and hanging on the side of the bus. The driver knew he was not going to win this one. I don't know how he warned them but when we arrived at the Recruit Depot we paid the piper. There were ten Shore Patrolmen waiting for us. We were ordered off the bus and herded into a large drill hall that was about the size of three basketball courts. During the winter months, drills outside were almost impossible because of the heavy snows. They stood us up in the middle of the drill hall and did not say another word to us. This was about 2200 (10:00 p.m. in civilian time). We stood there all night. We were not allowed to sit or move from our allotted space. At 0500 a chief petty officer came in and asked if any of us was interested in going for a bus ride. So began my second day in the Navy.

****

Anyone who has been through one of the military's basic training systems knows what a pain that experience is. Anyone who has not been through one would never understand, so there is no need to discuss it in detail. I do feel a need to explain that things were a lot different in the military of 1961 than they are today. Our Company Commander (CC) was an active duty first class petty officer and a Korean War veteran. He needed help from some of us recruits to ensure that things were done according to his and the Navy's requirements. He made recruit petty officer assignments based upon any prior military experience. Since I had served ever so briefly in the National Guard, I was assigned the position of the Boatswain Mate of the Watch. In that capacity I made up all the watch bills and stood no watches myself.

The most interesting assignment was the assignment of Master at Arms. The CC looked out over the company of approximately sixty recruits and found the biggest guy in the group. He brought him up front and after determining his name said, "Antoinette, you are my Master at Arms." Antoinette smiled. The CC asked him if he knew what that job entailed. Antoinette said, "No, Sir." The CC explained that he would be the enforcer of all the commands given by the CC and any of the senior recruit petty officers, and that he would get one additional recruit liberty.

Antoinette smiled. Then the CC asked if there was anyone in the Company who thought they would like to be the Master at Arms. A spark plug of a guy standing about 5'9" stepped forward and said that he thought he would like the job. The CC turned to Antoinette and asked if he wanted to give the job to the new guy. Antoinette said, "Hell no." The CC said, "It looks like we have a problem." Because of the wet snowy winters all the barracks had small drying rooms where hot dry air was forced through to dry our uniforms after we hand washed them. The CC suggested that Antoinette and the new guy go into the drying room and decide who was going to be the Master at Arms. As soon as the door was closed you could hear fists flying. After about five minutes, with a busted nose and a big grin on his face the spark plug stated, "I'm the Master at Arms." I knew at that moment that life in the Navy was not going to be a lark.

I made no lasting friends in boot camp and never saw one of my boot camp mates later in my career.

****

The most significant event in recruit training is classification day, when based upon scores from various test and the "needs of the Navy" you find out what job you will be doing after graduation. I was numb through most of the test from the previous day's grueling schedule but scored high enough to be assigned as a hospital corpsman. There were two "A" Schools that taught basic hospital corpsman courses. One was right there in Great Lakes, the other was in San Diego, California. Typical Navy logic: I was at Great Lakes but my orders for training were to San Diego.

After a short recruit leave of five days I caught a train from Columbia, S.C. to San Diego. The train ride was an adventure in and of itself. Before joining the Navy I had only been out of the state twice, once in a stolen car and once to visit my oldest sister who was married to a sailor and lived in Pensacola, Florida.

By the time I got to San Diego I was down to my last $.75 cents. In the train station I saw Sailors wandering around all over. I finally found one that did not look too intimidating and asked him where the naval base was located. He looked at me somewhat confused and asked, "Which one?" I asked, "How many are there?" "At least eight in the San Diego area," he told me. Knowing that I was really lost he asked to see my orders. When he saw them he said I was going to the naval hospital at Balboa, and gave me general directions. Wanting to save my little bit of change I threw my seabag over my shoulder and started to walk in the general direction he had pointed. After about fifteen blocks I started to look for a bus stop. While standing on the corner a car stopped and a chief petty officer driving asked where I was going. I told him Balboa Naval Hospital. He said, "Throw your seabag in the back seat and hop in. I'm going that way."

I did so and immediately upon getting into the front seat I knew something was wrong. The seat was wet. About that time he said, "Oh hell, I forgot my girlfriend got sick and threw up on the seat."

Well needless to say I made quite an impression when I reported to the Hospital Corps School at Balboa Naval Hospital. I smelled so bad that the petty officer that was checking me in would not let me come into his office. I had to slide my orders and records across the room to him. He told me where the barracks were and that there was someone there that would get me settled. The petty officer at the barracks was just as nice and accommodating as the previous one. He made me stand outside and he threw the bed linens out into the hall and gave me directions to my squad bay. Lucky for me there was no one in the area so I had time to get out of my smelly blues, grab my shaving kit and find the shower. I took the dress blues with me and washed the vomit out as best I could. Dress blues are 100% wool and smell like a wet dog when damp. But at least I didn't have to explain the smell.

****

Hospital Corps School was extremely difficult. I had to learn all the muscles, all the bones and all the organs in the human body and their functions. We had to learn to identify symptoms of various ailments and identify treatment plans for the problems. We learned to give shots by giving them to each other. We learned to draw blood and start intravenous medications by again doing it to each other. We learned to suture minor wounds. Although the course was tough, I did find that I had more freedom and had a chance to make a few friends. We would study together and go on liberty and drink together. The enlisted men's club was the least expensive place to drink so we spent a lot of time and money there.

After Corps School I was assigned to the Commander, U.S. Amphibious Forces, Pacific Fleet, at the Naval Amphibious Base on Coronado Island near San Diego. The Navy ran liberty boats from the Navy's 5th Street Landing in San Diego to the Naval Amphibious Base every thirty minutes. There was also a civilian ferry system that ran between San Diego and North Island. If you took the civilian ferry you were still about three miles from the amphibious base. When I reported in I was told that I would be working in the base clinic and told to report to Chief Bowers at the clinic. Things went fairly well to start with. I slowly began to understand that the senior enlisted and officer leadership was mostly made up of men who had served during WWII and Korea.

The Uniform Code of Military Justice was the governing system to deal with minor and major infractions of military law. Most of these senior enlisted and officers had served when the governing document was "Rocks and Shoals"—the informal name of the "Articles for the Government of the United States Navy." Justice under the Articles was swift, and tended to be harsh. The current system, "The Uniform Code of Military Justice," replaced Rocks and Shoals in 1951. But the old timers had a hard time adjusting to the new system so the old one was still frequently practiced. If you were told to do something and gave too much hesitation you could expect to be knocked on your butt. There were never any witnesses and the senior member was always believed if there were differing stories.

One morning while shaving in the washroom a junior hospital corpsman came in to shave and right behind him was a third class petty officer. Before I knew what was happening the petty officer punched the corpsman in the mouth and then in the stomach. There was a second class petty officer standing next to me shaving and he immediately looked the other way. I didn't know what to do, but the second class petty officer suggested that I look the other way as he was sure that I had seen nothing. Later the hospital corpsman went to the Master Chief to complain and the Master Chief called all of us together to get the story straight. Of course the third class who had administered the punches did not know what the corpsman was talking about. And when the second class said he had not seen anything it left me with a decision. I'm not the smartest guy in the world, but I'm also not stupid. I saw nothing.

****

During this tour I met a guy who would become a lifelong friend, Ron Davis. We spent a lot of our liberty hours exploring the San Diego area and when we had the money for drinks and women we headed to Tijuana, Mexico. Ron and I learned a lot about life in Tijuana. We also learned how to outrun the local police when we got into a situation that might result in us spending some time in a Tijuana jail. If we could out run them to the border, the U.S. officials were always accommodating in that they let us jump to the front of the line and get back on the U.S. side. Ron and I had a propensity to get ourselves into some interesting situations.

We bought a 1950 Ford that, although it was missing a back window, was fairly reliable. We started to go to Lake Arrowhead on our free weekends with another of our friends, Rodney Hanson. Rodney was a seaman with three hash marks and was our hero. At that time you earned a hash mark for every three years of service. So that meant that Rodney had over nine years of active duty. Interestingly he had never been busted. We should have known then that he was no Einstein, but he was our leader and we blindly followed his lead. He was the one that came up with going to Lake Arrowhead on the weekends. We got a job on Saturdays and Sundays cleaning up construction sites. We were allowed to room above the Lake Arrowhead Restaurant and Lounge in exchange for our bussing tables during the evening hours. Going to and from Lake Arrowhead was at times more of an adventure than we bargained for.

On one such trip we were on the way to Lake Arrowhead and had been drinking since we had left Coronado. On the way we noticed a female hitch-hiker and stopped and offered her a ride. Rodney was driving and I was riding shotgun. Ron was in the backseat with our new female friend. Ron made the mistake of trying to get too friendly with the hitch-hiker and she commenced to beat the living crap out of him. Even after he surrendered she continued to beat his ass. We finally had to stop and physically throw her out of the car.

On another trip we stopped at the side of a gas station to use the bathroom. When we got ready to leave we had the unfortunate event of running, broadside, into a beautiful Corvette. The body was fiberglass and we did a job on it. The young driver went nuts and finally Rodney knocked him on his butt. After that the driver went inside the gas station and called his dad. It seemed as if they were in the gas station the police arrived so fast. Rodney, Ron and I had been drinking for the past two hours and were in pretty bad shape.

All three of us were leaning against our car when the policeman in charge asked Rodney if he was the driver? Rodney said, "No, officer, I was in the back seat." I was next in line and as drunk as I was I knew that Rodney had lied because he was driving. When the officer asked me if I was driving, I quickly said, "No officer, I also was in the back seat." Well that left poor ole Ron to take the heat. The officer asked Ron, "Well I assume you were the driver?" Ron smiled and said, "No, officer, we were all in the backseat drinking beer." Within the next few minutes we were on our way to jail.

Once they determined we were military they contacted our base and the clinic Master Chief came up the next day and retrieved us from the local police. We paid a heavy price in extra duty for the next two months before the Master Chief decided we might now behave on liberty. We had car insurance and I assume they took care of the kid's Corvette.

On another trip to Lake Arrowhead we had a wreck with a small Renault. The driver was the daughter of a doctor in the local area. She was driving too fast and sideswiped a car in front of us and hit us head-on. We were stunned but not hurt. Not so with the two occupants of the Renault. Rodney took charge. "Hugh, you and I are going to see if we can assist these girls. Ron you throw all of the empty beer cans as far down the mountain as you can and the full ones close enough to the road that we can retrieve them later."

The passenger was hurt, but it did not look life threatening. The driver was obviously more seriously hurt. She was somewhat trapped under the steering wheel and the collapsed dash. We smelled gas and decided that we had to get her out of the car before a fire broke out. Getting her out was no simple task, but after Ron had completed his assigned task he gave us a hand and we were able to get her out of the car and away from the potential fire. The passenger was sitting against a tree next to where we placed the driver. Sure as hell the vehicle started to burn and then there was an explosion as the gas tank blew. Ron was the closest to the car and happened to be looking at the car when the explosion occurred. He had no facial hair and his face received first degree burns. Soon the police and two ambulances arrived. Both girls were hurt more than we were so they were loaded into the ambulances and left for the hospital. The car that the girls had sideswiped was the one who called the police and reported the accident. The police loaded us up in their squad cars and took us to the hospital for examination. With the exception of Jack's facial burns, we were in good enough shape that they released us. Once again the Master Chief found himself on the way to Lake Arrowhead to retrieve his favorite three nitwits.

The father sued us for moving his daughter because she had a fractured pelvis and he claimed we did permanent damage by moving her. Well our old sea daddy Rodney saw that this was a defensive move because she was at fault and dad was worried about us suing her/him. Rodney contacted a lawyer and explained the situation and the lawyer filed suit on our behalf. Within a month the whole thing was settled and Rodney, Ron, and I received a check from her insurance company in the amount of $500 each.

Lord knows giving us that much money with no supervision was sure to cause the local community some serious problems. Look out Tijuana there is going to be some serious liberty until the money runs out. It was all gone within three weeks. But, boy did we have some stories to tell.

THREE

T HREE MONTHS AFTER REPORTING TO THE CLINIC I found out why my orders were to the Amphibious Force, which probably ended up saving my life. One morning at muster (roll call) at the clinic, the Master Chief told me that I was to report to the Admin Office at Amphibious Force immediately. When I got there I was told to go to the barracks and pack my seabag and report back within one hour. I asked what was going on and was told to just go pack. When I reported back I was told that a ship was deploying for a Western Pacific (West Pac) cruise at 2:00 p.m. and they had lost one of their corpsmen. I was his replacement. I was assured that by the time the ship reached Pearl Harbor a relief would be waiting for me and I would be flown back to San Diego.

I reported to the USS *Talladega* (APA-208), a transport ship that was commissioned in June of 1945. She was primarily a troop transport ship. She was 255 feet long with a crew of 536 and could carry 1561 troops. We were transporting a load of Marines from Long Beach, California, to Okinawa. Then we would continue on to various ports in the Western Pacific and pick up passengers. Remembering from recruit training how to report aboard a ship I successfully made it to the quarter deck. The boatswain mate of the watch called sick bay and requested someone come fetch this newbie. A third class petty officer came up and led me to sick bay. He introduced me around and indicated that I would be assigned to a berth in one of the ship's berthing areas but that all of the enlisted corpsmen slept in sick bay. There were three empty bunks available and I chose one of the lower ones. He found out where I was to be berthed and took me down and helped me get settled. It was kind of nice having two places to sleep. The only time we slept in the berthing area was when we needed the bunks in sick bay for patients.

My new mentor was named Jim Harris. He was making his second, nine month West Pac cruise so I figured that I should stick close to him and learn from his experiences.

****

The smells and noises in a ship are something that takes some getting used to. Even when in port engines are running, equipment is being operated and there is nowhere that people are not giving orders or just socializing. After getting somewhat settled, Ron took me on a familiarization tour and introduced me to a lot of folks. He seemed to know everyone on the ship. He took great pains to lead me to and from sick bay to the chow hall, to the post office, the ship's office (where personal records are kept) and to the geedunk, a small store where you could buy most necessary items, candy, and cigarettes. Cigarettes were ten cents a pack or a buck a carton. There were very few places on the ship where one could not smoke.

Jim asked me if I got seasick. To be honest I did not know. I had never been to sea and the biggest floating object I had ever been in was a small wooden boat on a pond. He said if I found myself getting seasick to try to find a toilet and stay with it until I could get my stomach under control. He advised against going on the weather deck for the first two days as all the seasick Sailors and Marines on the ship would be there and the spray they put out was something to be avoided.

After the orientation tour Jim introduced me to the senior hospital corpsman onboard, Chief Brown. After reviewing my records, Chief Brown explained that there were ten corpsmen assigned to the *Talladega* and that he and the first class petty officer did not stand watches. The remaining eight of us stood port and starboard when at sea and we stood a four section watch when in port. What that meant was that when at sea I had the duty every other day and when in a port I had the duty once every four days. At sea the duty was not much as we were all onboard and most of us spent 90% of our time in sick bay anyway. Since I was the junior member of the department I had the honor of rising at 4:30 a.m. every morning and being at the galley to receive from the baker a tray of today's sweet rolls, donuts or whatever sweets they had made during the night. This was a valuable lesson for me. I found that there was a lot of back scratching onboard ships. The "Docs," as we were all referred to, were in the upper tier of the folks getting their backs scratched.

****

To my delight I found that I was not prone to seasickness. In fact the movement did not bother me at all. I took every opportunity to learn my trade as a hospital corpsman. There were the usual colds, flu and such to deal with at sick call, but when an injured Sailor or Marine came to sick bay I always tried to get the Chief or the doctor to let me take care of it. I learned quickly that when suturing a wound I had the option of trying to make the future scar as small as possible or as large as I wanted it to be. I frequently asked, especially Marines with facial wounds, if they wanted to look rugged or pretty. Most Marines opted for the bigger scar.

When we got to Pearl Harbor, Hawaii, the Pacific Fleet Band was playing on the pier. I felt like a real hero being welcomed home from the wars. There were a lot of supplies waiting for us and a good bit of mail. What was not there was my relief. After three days in Pearl and two opportunities to do some sightseeing we were underway again. I did not see a single Hawaiian girl in a grass skirt.

Our next stop was Midway Island, a 2.4 square mile interesting and historic island. One of the most important battles of the Second World War was fought there. This battle, won by the U.S., was the turning point in the war against Japan. Midway is also famous for the world's largest albatross, commonly called the Gooney Bird. These birds spend their breeding season on Midway and then fly away to God knows where until the following breeding season. They are very graceful in the air but have not mastered the art of landing. When they land, mostly on the runway, they go ass over tea kettle down the runway until their momentum stops them. Their take-off is also interesting. They need almost two-thirds of the runway to get a running start, flapping their wings to get airborne. Because there are so many Gooneys living there during breeding season, when a plane is scheduled to land Sailors in pick-up trucks line up at one end of the runway and slowly drive its length while Sailors in the back reach out and grab the birds by the neck and put them in the back of the pick-up. Then they take them to an area where they can control them until the plane makes its landing.

We were only at Midway for two days and then on to Wake Island. Again, not much to describe about an island that small, but it was and is important to the U.S.

We stopped at Okinawa to debark our Marine passengers and were there for four days.

Okinawa is located in southern Japan. It consists of hundreds of the Ryukyu Islands in a chain over 620 miles long, which extends southwest from Kyushu (the southwestern most of Japan's main four islands) to Taiwan. Okinawa's capital, Naha, is located in the southern part of Okinawa Island. In 1962 Okinawa was still a U.S. possession and the people drove on the right side of the road as we did in the U.S. I found the Okinawans to be very courteous. They spoke Japanese, but with their own dialect.

By the time we got there the old hands on the ship had me convinced that the Japanese women's genitalia ran sideways, rather than vertical like our women. I could not wait to get a look at these strangely constructed women. Lies, lies, and damn lies. Nothing was different other than the women were, generally speaking, smaller in stature than our round-eyed love ones back home. This was my first experience with Asians and especially Asian women. They were not bashful at all and their community toilets and baths were open to all. Their sexuality was very open and they did not get embarrassed when their bodies were exposed. This behavior took some getting used to.

We picked up some fifty-odd Marines and a couple of Sailors. They sure had their pick of the berthing area, being such a small number. The two Sailors were Fleet Marine corpsmen so they were relegated to the troop berthing area with the Marines.

Next stop: Yokosuka, Japan. It only took one trip to the "hotsee" bath to make a believer out of me. That was one of the most relaxing experiences of my life and that is where I learned to love a good massage. I also learned to love oriental food during this cruise. Unlike some cities in Japan, Yokosuka was only bombed infrequently during WWII, the most significant bombing being during the Doolittle raid. It was bombed periodically by U. S. Navy planes, but not much damage was inflicted.

Next stop: Hong Kong. I had long forgotten that a relief was supposed to be running around the Pacific trying to catch up with the ship and let me fly home. Besides, I was having a ball. We worked long hard hours when at sea but the learning experience was great. Hong Kong is one of the most interesting cities in the world. There were people of every nationality in Hong Kong, but mostly Chinese and they spoke mostly Chinese. I learned that we had a money expert on the ship and that I could invest in his trade of working the money exchanges in Hong Kong. The money expert was a chief petty officer who had no shipboard duties while in Hong Kong and seemed to be able to come and go as he pleased. I suspect that not only enlisted were investing with the Chief, but so were the officers. I invested $20 with him and either got a return or a loss, based upon my share of the total amount he had to start with. He did well most of the time, and after three days he returned my $20 plus $8 more.

From Hong Kong we sailed for Naval Base Subic Bay in the Philippines. Subic Bay was a major Navy ship-repair, supply and rest and recreation facility located in Olongapo, Zambales, Philippines. The Navy exchange there had the largest volume of sales of any exchange in the world, and the Naval Supply Depot handled the largest volume of fuel oil of any navy facility in the world. The naval base was the largest overseas military installation of the United States Armed Forces.

The Philippines has a rich and varied history. The Spanish were the first Westerners to occupy the Philippines and that would explain the appearance of the people. I was surprised when I went ashore and found that the Filipino people were not oriental, but more Spanish looking. They were a good looking people and the women were beautiful. The people spoke a local dialect called Tagalog but most could also communicate in Spanish and English.

In 1898 during the Spanish American War, Commodore Dewey

attacked and destroyed the Spanish fleet in the battle of Subic Bay. The battle started with Commodore Dewey's famous order to Charles Gridley, of the Olympia: "You may fire when you are ready, Gridley."

During WWII the Japanese attacked and successfully occupied the Philippines until the return of General Douglas MacArthur and the subsequent battles that drove the Japanese from the Philippines. This period of Philippine history fills many books, so no need to get into details with my story.

The liberty place in Subic was Olongapo. Olongapo was a sailor's dream. The women were beautiful, the booze cheap and the law enforcement almost non-existent. There is no sailor that has ever been to Olongapo that does not have at least a dozen or more stories to tell. Every night was a new adventure and worthy of keeping for later telling during "story time" at sea. While most of us came back to the ship with no money we rarely felt that we had not gotten our money's worth during the liberty.

Sadly we had to say goodbye to the Philippines where we had picked up an additional eighty-plus Sailors and Marines headed back to the States.

We made our next to last stop on our way back home. We stopped at the naval base at Taipei, Taiwan. The people of Taiwan were Chinese and mostly refugees from mainland China as a result of civil war that broke out after WWII. Liberty amounted to one night ashore and was mostly uneventful. We picked up a handful of Sailors and one Marine. The berthing compartments were still far from full.

Our final stop was back at White Beach in Okinawa. Since we had been there already we knew where the action was—Gate Two Street outside of the Kadena Air Force Base. This street was one long street of nothing but bars. The action was fast and the cost low, so we had our share of problems with ship's company and local Shore Patrol and Ryukyu Police. If I recall we left two of our ship's company Sailors in the custody of either the Shore Patrol or the Ryukyu Police.

When we landed at San Diego after a nine month absence I felt like a true fleet sailor. To my surprise my relief was waiting on the pier and reported aboard as soon as the gangplank was in place. I was told to report back to U.S. Naval Amphibious Forces Command Headquarters (PhibPac). I departed the ship with trepidation. I had learned to consider the U.S.S. *Talladega* as home and the crew as part of my extended family.

****

Well I certainly got a shock when I reported back to PhibPac Headquarters. The Chief of Staff personally welcomed me back and informed me that I was to call my detailer (Assignment Chief Petty Officer). I knew this was not a good thing, but had no choice. I was allowed to call my detailer from one of the administrative offices and he too welcomed me home and informed me that my sea duty was not up. All along I thought I was on shore duty when in fact I was assigned to PhibPac as a supernumerary and my West Pac tour was a good example of why they needed supernumeraries. The detailers were broken up into three different groups all reporting to the Bureau of Naval Personnel. One assigned personnel to the West Coast Fleet and foreign shores of the Pacific, one assigned personnel to the East Coast Fleet and foreign shores of the Atlantic, the third, and the one everyone wanted to deal with, was the one that assigned personnel to shore assignments in the U.S.

My detailer really sent me for a loop when he informed me that I was being assigned to the Third Marine Division on Okinawa. But first I had to go through Field Medical Service School training at Camp Delmar, near Camp Pendleton, California. I was given five days leave between checking out of PhibPac and reporting to Field Medical Service School. I could hardly go home to South Carolina and be back within five days, so I decided to spend a couple of days with my friends at the base clinic and then go to Field Medical Service School a little early.

To my surprise and dismay my friend Ron was no longer there. Ron was aboard an aircraft carrier and Rodney had been discharged due to medical reasons. I never found out what the medical reasons were and never saw Rodney again.

Dejected, I went to the barracks and packed the remainder of my meager belongings. I was paid $76 a month and one does not tend to collect many belongings on that pay.

I caught the ferry going to the Fifth Street Landing the next morning and caught a bus from there to the Greyhound bus station where I purchased a ticket to Oceanside, California, which was as close as I could get to Camp Del Mar. I caught a taxi to the main gate at Camp Del Mar and was instructed where to report for Field Medical Service School.

FOUR

I LEARNED ANOTHER VALUABLE LESSON UPON CHECKING IN, never, never check into a duty station early, especially a training facility.

I was assigned to a barracks where I was the only sailor. It did not take long for me to find myself the brunt of what the Marines who lived in the barracks considered great fun. I was in the lobby trying to call home to inform the family of my latest assignment when four of the biggest guys I had ever seen came down the steps. They saw this sailor in the phone booth and came straight for me. One placed his foot against the folding doors so that I could not escape. Then the other three commenced to cut the phone line and between the four of them they laid the phone booth on the floor with the doors against the floor. I was entombed in a phone booth. I thought that they would let me suffer for a bit and then let me out. Surprise, surprise—they just walked out the front door and left me there. After a few minutes I started to scream hoping someone would come to my rescue. I lay in that damn phone booth for almost two hours before a Marine Corps captain came in the front doors and saw my situation. He was so black he looked almost blue. He was thin and muscular. I could tell that he could hold his own in almost any physical situation. At first he just stood with his hands on his hips and laughed at me. Then I think he began to feel sorry for me and he rolled the phone booth over on one side and helped me get out. He saw that I was a corpsman and asked if I was reporting to Field Medical Service School. I replied in the affirmative and he said that I should make myself scarce until I could report to the school tomorrow. Still three days early.

The first thing I did after being released from the phone booth was find the Field Medical Service School. It was late and only a staff sergeant was available. I told him that I was reporting into the school. He asked me where my gear was located. When I told him, he looked at me kind of strange and said that was a bad move. I replied that I had already found that out. When I told him what had happened with the phone booth I thought he would piss his pants laughing. He said that I needed to go get my gear and he would put me up in the right barracks. He also said that I probably needed a bodyguard to go back over and get my gear. He locked the door to the building and went with me. The trip was uneventful in that we did not encounter any Marines. On the way back I asked him about locking the building and just leaving. He said that the chance of anyone important coming around at that time of the night was remote and that if someone called after his return questioning why he did not answer the phone earlier he would just tell them he heard the phone but was taking a crap and could not get to the phone.

My lesson about reporting in early continued. At 05:00 the next morning I was awakened by a gunny sergeant screaming in my ear, "Off your ass and on your feet!" I almost knocked him down getting out of the rack. I jumped to attention and he quite sternly said, "You dumbass. You don't stand at attention for enlisted personnel." Hell I had no idea what to do so I just stood there like the dumbass that I was. He smiled and said that I had twenty minutes to shit, shower and shave and report back to him at the admin office. I grabbed my shaving kit and headed to the shower. I took a shower in less than three minutes and shaved so fast that my face was cut up so badly that I looked like I had been in a knife fight. Forget the shit; just go see what this monster has in store for me.

I reported to the admin office and a corporal was sitting at the desk where I had met the staff sergeant the night before. I told him I was looking for a gunny sergeant that had told me to report to the admin office. I was informed that the Gunny had gone to breakfast and had left orders for me to do the same and to be back no later than 06:00. I asked for directions to the chow hall and fortunately it was less than one block away. Looking at my watch that gave me twenty-five minutes to go there, eat and return to the admin office. I didn't think I was going to eat much with that little bit of time.

I arrived at the chow hall just as a company of what I thought was

Marines were arriving. But, they were actually a part of the current class at Field Medical Service School. I was to get in line behind them. There were about fifty of them and I knew that there would be no breakfast that morning. So I just went back to the admin office. The corporal could not believe that I had eaten that fast. I told him that I was a very fast eater.

A few minutes later the Gunny returned and he asked if I owned running shoes and shorts. I said that I did not. He smiled and said, "No problem, come with me." I followed him to what obviously was a clothing issue room. He banged on the door and a corporal open the top half of the door and smiling said, "What can I do for you, Gunny?" The Gunny instructed the corporal to issue me a pair of combat boots with socks and three pair of athletic shorts. I had to fill out a form accepting receipt for the boots, socks, and shorts. The Gunny then looked at me smiling and said, "Meet me on the front steps in ten minutes."

I was not used to these short time fuse requirements, but started to understand that most orders were going to give me little time to think, just time to react.

In less than ten minutes I was standing on the front steps in combat boots and shorts. A minute or two later the Gunny came through the door and said, "Come with me. We're going for a little run." He started down the street at a pretty good pace, but I was able to keep up with him. All of a sudden he turned a corner and there was the ocean with a nice sandy beach. I thought, as he headed for the beach, that this is not going to be fun.

We had not gone a hundred yards when I started to lag behind. Running in sand with combat boots is almost impossible. However, the Gunny did not seem to be having any problem. After about a half a mile I stopped and decided that I had had enough. He was about 300 yards ahead of me and to my amazement he was running back to me. He said, "We are not going to stop and rest until we have completed our run." I just looked at him and shook my head. He said, "This is not an option, asshole." I got to my feet and with great effort tried to start running again. Looking at my watch I saw that it was only 0815 and the heat of the sun was already unbearable. I made it for about another half a mile before I stopped and threw up. I don't know where the upchuck came from because I had not eaten in almost twenty-four hours. He waited patiently and when it was obvious that I had nothing else to bring up he said, "Good, now we can get on with our run."

I knew that I was going to die that day because we had well over three more miles to go and I had quit twice and puked twice in the first one-plus miles.

Somehow I finished the run, though not of sound mind or strong heart. I was babbling when he asked me questions. He took me into the shade of a tree and walked over to what was obviously a prepositioned canteen of water. He brought the canteen to me and said, "Drink it slowly or you'll just throw it back up." After about an hour recovering he came back to the tree and said, "Go get a shower and head to the barber shop and get a regulation haircut. Then report to the uniform issue room."

I stumbled to the squad bay where I was assigned and got my shaving kit and went to the shower. The shower seemed to help revive me a little. I put my Navy uniform back on and went to the barber shop and then to the uniform issue room. The top half of the door was open and the corporal was smiling. He asked me if I had enjoyed my run. Knowing it was the wrong thing to do, but unable to help myself, I said, "Fuck you." He laughed and said, "You'll get used to it." He handed me a seabag full of Marine uniforms and told me that I should take them up and lay them out on my bunk and he would be up later to help me get organized.

When the corporal arrived I had everything laid out on my bunk, everything from green socks to green underwear. He gave me a sheet of paper that showed how everything was to be stored in my footlocker at the foot of my bunk. The sheet showed me how each item was to be folded and in what order they should be stored in the footlocker. I thought this is not the Navy. To my surprise the corporal walked me through the entire process. This was the only thing that was positive about reporting in early. I got a jump on the other classmates who would not have the benefit of the corporal's tutoring.

After placing everything in the footlocker, properly folded and in its proper place, the corporal picked out various articles and told me to get dressed. He left and I commenced the transformation from a Navy corpsman to a Fleet Marine Force corpsman. I briefly remember the two Fleet Marine corpsmen that we had picked up on my West Pac trip and how they had not been invited to join us in sick bay but were berthed in the area where the Marines were berthed. I had not thought much about it at the time because I didn't understand that there is quite a difference between a Fleet corpsman and a Fleet Marine corpsman.

I went back to the admin office after getting dressed and could feel the difference with which the Marines were now looking at me. While not yet trained, I was now becoming one of them. The difference between me and them was our physical appearance. There was not an ounce of fat on any of the Marines. Their uniforms were flawless and they all wore them with great pride.

****

The Gunny was in the office and asked me if I had received my complete uniform issue. I did not know how to respond but said "I think so." He smiled and said, "How many sets of workout shorts were you issued"? I told him I had three and they issued me one more pair. He said, "Then you have the complete issue."

"Do you know why you were issued four sets of workout shorts"? he said.

"No, Sir," I replied.

He jumped to his feet and screamed, "I am not a 'sir'! My parents were married. Don't ever refer to me or any other enlisted Marine as sir; we take great offense to that!"

"Yes, Sir."

The corporal broke up and the Gunny just shook his head. "The reason for four is that you will wear three each day and wash them at the end of the day," the Gunny continued. "Then you will wear the fourth on the following morning and the other three will be dry for use the rest of that day." It didn't take me long to learn that asking questions irritated gunny sergeants. I asked, "What will we be doing that will mess up three sets of workout shorts?" With a look of frustration he said, "They are workout shorts and you will be working out!" He then said for me to go to lunch and be back at 13:00 in my workout shorts and combat boots.

I headed for the galley and to my surprise I got there before the class going through training. In spite of the fact that I had not eaten in almost twenty-four hours I was not real hungry. They were serving cold cuts and soup. The soup was something I had never tasted, but was not bad. I had two bowls and headed back to the barracks. I had a few minutes before 13:00 so I went and tried to take a crap. No luck. I put on my workout shorts and combat boots and went back down to the admin office. The Gunny was waiting for me.

"How about a little run to help settle your lunch?" he said.

I thought, *Oh God don't do this to me twice in one day*! But being the smart ass that I am, I said, "I'll race you to the beach." Before I could move he was out the door. I knew that I could not catch him and even if I did I could not keep up with him.

Surprisingly I made it a little further before my lunchtime soup came up. I thought, my God I'm going to starve to death before I get out of this place. This time the Gunny did not come back for me and with every ounce of energy I pushed on. When I finished the five miles and got back to the admin office the Gunny was there in full uniform looking as if he had never left the building. He smiled and asked if I had finished the run or had I cheated. I said to him, "Gunny I can be an asshole at times and might even stretch the truth to enhance a good sea story, but I don't cheat and I don't lie." He looked at me kind of funny and said, "Good enough. Be ready before the evening meal to join me for another little jaunt."

I was about to say something that was sure to get me in trouble when the corporal yelled, "Attention on deck!" As I snapped to attention the Marine captain that had rescued me from the phone booth came through the front door. He said in a deep voice, "Carry on." He saw the Gunny and asked if he was taking care of me. The Gunny assured him that I was in his loving care and that he would ensure that I benefited from the quality time he was spending with me. The captain smiled and went into an inner office.

My class was to begin in two more days and I spent those two days in the "loving care" of the Gunny. It was almost as if he had taken me on to see just how long I could last. Later I asked the corporal at the front desk if it was just me or was the Gunny trying to kill me. He laughed and said,

"The Gunny loves people who do not give up. If he didn't like you he would have you doing crappy details around the base instead of giving you a hand up on the rest of your class when they arrive day after tomorrow."

I survived the next two days and actually got a little further on each of our three a day runs. I still could not finish without walking for a little while, but I could see that I was going to be able to master the physical aspects of this training.

The rest of my class arrived a few at a time until the last of them came in about 2000 the night before the class was to start. I could look at them and tell they had no idea what they were in for and that I was not even sure if some would make it through the physical portion of the class.

****

The next morning at 0430 the Gunny turned the lights on in the squad bay and screamed, "Off your ass and on your feet!" There were a few grumbles and then he shouted, "If I hear another word you will be doing push-ups all day. Now get dressed and get your asses out in front of the building in fifteen minutes!"

I put on my Marine uniform and smartly headed for the front door. I could tell by the looks I was getting that they were curious about what I was wearing. They put on their Navy Blues and followed me out the door. We kind of milled around until the Gunny came out and in his commanding voice said, "Okay shitheads, line up in four ranks." We continued to mill around until he screamed, "What the fuck are you idiots doing? Didn't the Navy teach you how to form ranks"? We were in four rows and facing the building in about fifteen seconds. The Gunny called, "Attenhut!" and we all popped to. We were not sure what was to happen next, but shortly the black Marine captain came out the front doors and just stood on the top step and looked at us. He introduced himself as Captain Leggett. He said that he was the senior Marine assigned to Field Medical Service School and that when we were not in medical training we belonged to him. With that, he turned and returned to the building.

The Gunny smiled and said, "You folks are going to wish you had never met this captain." He informed the class that this was the first and only morning that they would be allowed to eat chow prior to physical fitness. He looked around and finally his eyes stopped on me. "Seaman Sullivan," he said, "you will march this rag tag group to morning chow and have them back here in forty-five minutes."

Holy crap, I had never been in charge of marching anyone anywhere. I knew that any rebuttal would not be fun to watch. I stepped out front and to the left of the formation and ordered, "Left face. Forward, march." Thank God there were only two turns between the barracks and the chow hall. When we reached the chow hall I told them that they had thirty-five minutes to eat and be back outside and in formation. Then one rank at a time I led them to the chow hall entrance. To my surprise they were back outside and in formation when I came out about thirty-seven minutes later. I marched them back to the admin building and put them at ease. I then entered the building looking for the Gunny. He was waiting for me and congratulated me on my marching abilities. He told me that the first order was to get them to the barbershop and then to clothing issue. I looked at him strangely and he said, "Well, get a move on." I said, "Aye, aye" and promptly went out and marched my charges to the barbershop and from there to uniform issue. More and more my classmate were wondering what my position in all of this was. They knew that I was a sailor because I wore the Navy medical caduceus on my left collar point and the rank of a seaman on the right collar point.

After uniform issue the class was returned to the barracks and given the two sheets of paper that showed them how to fold each item and how to store each item in their footlockers. There was no corporal around to provide guidance and before I could begin to help the admin corporal came and got me. He said, "The Gunny wants to see you."

When I came in the company office following the corporal the Gunny said, "You don't need to lead them in getting squared away, go to the exchange and buy something." I knew that what he was doing was purposefully letting them suffer and make an effort to get things straight before he lit into them for not doing things right. What he was also doing was causing me a good bit of grief. The entire class was beginning to look at me with animosity.

I went to the geedunk and had a soda and then walked around the exchange for a few minutes and bought a can of shaving cream.

When I returned to the barracks the corporal on watch at the desk kindly suggested that I not go up topside as the Gunny was inspecting the efforts of the class to fold and store their gear and that from the rage he heard coming from the Gunny, things were not going so well. I decided to stay down below and chat with the corporal. About fifteen minutes later the Gunny came down the ladder (Navy for steps) and said, "Go up there and see if you can make heads or tails out of what those idiots are doing." When I arrived in the squad bay I was almost afraid to open my mouth. Gear was scattered all over the place, on the deck, on bunks even half way out of windows. Every soul there just stood as if shell shocked. It didn't take but a minute for them to notice me. I thought, "Oh crap, they are going to take this all out on me!"

One of the corpsmen mustered up the courage to address me and asked, "Just what the fuck is your status around here"? I decided that I needed to be honest and try to gain their favor. I explained that I was one of their classmates but that I had reported three days earlier. I had already been put through this and I guess that is why the Gunny is not giving me as much crap. I explained that if they wanted me to I would try to help them get their gear properly folded and stored. I first took them to my footlocker and showed them what the final product was supposed to look like.

Then I suggested that they sort out the items scattered all over the place by like items and then we would try to match the items up with the individuals based upon sizes. Working together, they got that accomplished within the hour. Then I had them gather around one of the bunks and watch as I folded each item. As I folded an item I would have each of them fold the same item. I was having them fold the items in the order that they would be placed in their footlocker. It took about two hours but we finally had everything properly folded and stored in its proper place.

I then went back down below and the corporal said that the Gunny told him that when I came back down to have me come over to the admin office. When I got to the admin office the Gunny was coming out the door. He asked me if I had them squared away. I smiled and said, "Gunny

I don't know if some of them will ever get squared away." He laughed and said for me to go back to the squad bay and get them all into Utility uniforms and have them in formation in front of the barracks in half an hour. A half an hour was cutting it close but I decided to get them dressed the same way I had gotten them to fold and store their uniforms, one item at a time. We were in formation and standing a parade rest when the Gunny arrived.

It was about 1430 and he told them that the first six weeks of training would be focused on medical training of combat injuries. The last two weeks we would be transferred over to Camp Pendleton where every effort would be made to teach us how to stay alive in a combat situation and how to live as a Marine lives in the field. He told them that they could expect to do a lot of running during all phases of the training. We would run three times a day, before breakfast, before lunch and before dinner. What he did not tell them was where and how long we would be running. He said that reveille was at 04:30 each morning and that we would be lined up in formation in front of the barracks no later than 05:00 in combat boots and running shorts. After our little run they would take a shower, get dressed and be out front ready to march to the chow hall by 0730. Then we would be turned over to the medical staff for training at 08:15 daily. He then said, "I know it is a little early but I think we should do our pre-dinner run now. Get into your running shorts and combat boots and be back in formation in fifteen minutes."

That first run was memorable. When we hit the beach sand, folks started to fall. I was somewhat surprised to see the Marine captain leading the run. The amazing thing was he was running backwards and cursing us every step of the way. For the first time I finished the run without stopping. I think my motivation was that if the captain was going to do it backwards then I damn sure was going to finish it frontwards. I was the only corpsman to finish the run. The Gunny was waiting at the finish and smiled when he saw me finish. I did not know it but there were several corporals following in the sand and two ambulances with a doctor and three corpsmen riding the road watching to ensure that if anyone got into serious trouble help was nearby.

When it was time to form up for our march to chow, there were about a third fewer of us than before. The Gunny told me to hold the formation in place until he returned. When he returned, the remainder of my charges were with him. We made it to chow and then back to the barracks. Most wanted nothing but to lie down. Some were praying that they would have a heart attack or a stroke during the night because they knew that tomorrow was going to be worse. No one was allowed to lie on his bunk before 2100 at night. So most just rested on the floor by their bunk and tried to ease the sore muscles in their entire body.

A couple of the guys came over and sat next to me. I did not know what to expect. To my surprise they asked me how I was able to complete the run. I told them that I had a three day head start on them and that I had done no better on my first run. I also told them that I was fast beginning to realize that a lot of this physical stuff was as much mental as physical. You had to force the pain from your mind and focus on something else. One asked me what I focused on today. I told him that I decided that for every step the Marine captain took backwards I was going to match going forward. It kept my mind off of the pain. Today was my eleventh run and the first that I had finished without stopping.

The daily torture continued but most of us endured and the medical training was tough but fascinating. We practiced on dummies and on people wearing moulages which looked like actual injuries. Our instructors were senior Fleet Marine corpsmen and physicians, most of them with actual combat experience. We learned and we practiced, and eventually got proficient enough that the staff was ready to pass us on at the end of the six weeks of medical training—and physical abuse of running in the sand three times a day. Of the fifty that started the course thirty-eight moved on to the Marine phase of our training.

The Gunny met with us for the last time on the day of departure to Camp Pendleton. At morning muster he passed out a sheet that listed everything that should be packed in our backpacks for long distance marching. Everything else was to be stored in our seabag and taken to the uniform issue room where it would be trucked to our new quarters. He ordered us to be back in front of the barracks wearing our backpacks and 782 gear (a harness-like device that held our canteens, medical pouches, etc.).

I took this opportunity to stop the Gunny and ask him his name. He asked, "Why do you want to know?" I said so that later when we ran across each other again I would know whose ass I was kicking. He laughed and said, "Fair enough, my name is Henderson." I knew that I would never forget this incredible Marine.

FIVE

Y OU DO NOT HAVE TO BE A ROCKET SCIENTIST TO KNOW that we were going to march from Camp Delmar to Camp Pendleton. I had been to Camp Pendleton and knew that it was one heck of a distance from the front gate to the first building. The distance was about fifteen miles, but we made it to the front gate intact. The corporal that I had always thought of as the admin guy was in charge of us during the march.

I was surprised, but then maybe not, when the corporal turned us off the paved road inside Camp Pendleton's main gate and marched us down a little two-lane rut of a road in the direction of some distant mountains. After about a five hour march we turned a corner in the road and could see a tent city ahead of us. No barracks life in the near future. The camp was mainly made up of general purpose tents (G.P.'s). The G.P. large tent was 18' wide by 52' long (a 936 sq. ft. footprint) by 5'6" eaveline and 12' ridgeline height. The tent features four windows on each sidewall and one screened doorway at each end. The entire sidewall rolls and ties in the up position for flow through ventilation. Normally when used for berthing these tents would accommodate sixteen people with their personal gear.

We were assigned to specific tents and then marched to a large tent that served as the mess hall. We used our personal mess gear and went through the mess line with our mess kits held out for the servers to slop whatever was being served. We then went to the other side of the tent and received Kool-Aid in our canteen cups. We were allowed thirty minutes to eat and be back in formation in front of our respective tents.

California weather can be trying on the body. The daytime highs often approached 100 degrees and the nighttime lows could drop into the forties. That afternoon we were marched to a set of bleachers that were cut into the side of a hill with wooden planks laid on the ground. It was explained to us that we were now entering into the Marine phase of our Fleet Marine Force training. We would be taught everything we would need to know in order to survive duty with the Marines. We would learn to march in uneven terrain with full combat gear that weighed from seventy to eighty pounds. We would learn to field strip, clean and reassemble the infantryman's main weapon—the M-14 rifle. Though it was unwieldy in the thick brush due to its length and weight, the power of the 7.62 mm NATO cartridge allowed it to penetrate cover quite well and reach out to extended ranges.

We also learned to field strip, clean and reassemble the M-1911 A1 .45-caliber pistol. The M-1911 served as the standard-issue side arm for the United States Armed Forces from 1911 to 1985. We learned to read a compass, shoot an azimuth and find our way to any point on a map. Mostly we lived as the Marines live in the field and learned to survive with meager personal comforts.

This period of our training lasted seventeen days. On day fifteen we were marched ten miles to the infiltration course. This course was composed of unruly terrain with bunkers placed periodically throughout. There was barbed wire placed over the entire course and was only two feet above the ground. The object was for us to begin at one end of the course and survive live fire that was being fired just about two inches above the barbed wire. We were to traverse this course on our backs with our M-14s on our chest. The length of the course was about seventy-five yards. The bunkers were loaded with live charges that were periodically exploded as we traversed the course. I found out early that one should stay as far away from the bunkers as possible because when one of the charges went off it would actually cause you to leave the ground and therefore bring you closer to the live fire going over your head.

It rarely rains in Southern California, but it had rained steadily for two days prior to our trip to the infiltration course. The mud was four to six inches deep throughout the entire course. Somehow, we all successfully survived.

Full of mud from head to toe we were marched another three miles to a barracks. However, we were informed that we would not be allowed to enter the barracks until the mud was removed. The Marines are never at a loss for solutions. Within ten minutes a fire truck pulled up in front of the barracks and a hose was attached to a fire hydrant. We stripped down to nothing and were hosed down. We then went into the barracks and brought a fifty-five-gallon galvanized trash can outside to transport our muddy clothes into the showers where we washed them. We also sat in the showers and field stripped our M-14s and with toothbrushes cleaned them. It had been a miserable day that was about to get more miserable.

While we were trying to get our gear squared away our captain came into the squad bay and requested silence. We knew that something bad was about to be shared with to us. The captain reported that President Kennedy had been assassinated in Dallas, Texas. This was the 22nd of November, 1963. We were in shock. No one knew what to say or do. The captain was emotionally taken by this event, but in true Marine fashion he told us that we should continue with our chores and be ready to march to chow in one hour.

SIX

WE WERE SCHEDULED TO GRADUATE THE FOLLOWING MONDAY, the 25th, and then given ten days leave on our way to our next duty station. I and a young Mexican kid named Juan, from the Los Angeles area, were the only two headed to the Third Marine Division in Okinawa. Juan asked me if I was going to go the South Carolina on my leave. I had enough money to buy a train ticket or a bus ticket but not enough to fly. The train or the bus was a two day trip each way leaving me with six days at home. I decided that I would just go ahead and check in for transportation to Okinawa. Juan invited me to spend a few days with him at his home and then he would go early with me to Okinawa. I was not very familiar with the Mexican culture but decide what the heck, why not? His father met us at the front gate and after introductions we were on our way. I not only had found a new best friend, but I found that Mexican food was second only to Southern cooking. His mother was determined to fatten us up before we left for Okinawa. Juan's parents were very nice to me and his younger brother was under foot everywhere we went for four days. I went to a phone booth and called home to let Mom and Dad know that I would not be coming home until after my thirteen month tour in Okinawa. They were disappointed, but said they understood.

We stayed with Juan's parents for three days and then caught a Greyhound to Treasure Island, California. We reported to the Transient Personnel Office and presented our orders. We were told that we would be there for about three to four days and then we would be transported to Travis Air Force Base where we would fly to Okinawa.

We were told that we would have the duty every other day as long as we were there. Juan and I were able to get assigned to the same duty roster. When not on duty we were free to go on liberty.

My duty turned out to be what was referred to as "roving patrol" and was performed from 2100 until 0600. When I reported the first night I was given a web belt that had a clipboard attached with several sheets of printed material, a nightstick and a flashlight that had batteries so weak that I could not even read the printed material on the clipboard. My patrol involved marching around the commissary and the exchange complex. The first class petty officer warned me that the patrol I was going to be performing was at times dangerous. In fact one sailor was hospitalized from an incident that took place during his watch. I was warned to be especially careful around the two big trailers behind the commissary.

I found out later that a great big sailor was on the same patrol that I was to stand and he heard something moving around the trailers. When he went to investigate he was hit in the chest with something. Turned out that something was alive! He immediately began to beat the living crap out of whatever it was with his night stick. As it turned out it was a cat that was trying to stay warm near the generators from the trailers, and when the sailor startled it, the cat jumped and got its front paw caught in the sailor's P-Coat. By the time the cat was dislodged the sailor had one black eye and got his two front teeth knocked out.

****

The Exchange is like a large department store and the Commissary is a big grocery store. My guess was that there had been some items stolen from one or the other so they felt it necessary to guard them at night. I was instructed to wear my field jacket as it tended to get cold at nights. Cold, hell; I almost froze to death! I found the two large tractor trailers with cold goods stored in them and they had a generator running to keep the items inside cold. The cat was smart, these generators put out a little heat. Needless to say I spent most of my patrolling as close to those generators as I could. I survived the night.

The next morning, with no sleep, Juan and I got dressed and headed to San Francisco. Juan had been to San Francisco twice with his parents visiting relatives in the area so he knew where to go. We headed straight to the wharf in the waterfront area. I was amazed at how busy and exciting that area was. We also had lunch, eating crab and crab soup. We rode the streetcar up to the main business district and promptly rode it back down to the waterfront. Later we ate dinner at the Buena Vista Café, purported to be the first place in the U.S. to serve Irish Coffee. We had a hamburger and a beer.

When we reported back to Treasure Island we were told that transportation to Travis Air Force Base would be provided at 0900 the next morning.

The air terminal at Travis was like a civilian terminal. We checked in with the Military Liaison Officer and were told not to leave the area. We found room on one of the many wooden benches and commenced to wait. About two hours later there was an announcement requesting that Seaman Sullivan report to the Liaison Office, that he had a guest waiting for him. I knew that I knew no one in the area so I assumed that there was more than one Seaman Sullivan in the terminal. Well the announcement continued at ten minute intervals. I finally decided to go to the Liaison Office and make sure they were not looking for me.

BIG MISTAKE! When I reported, the Air Force sergeant there was somewhat pissed off that I had not responded earlier. I tried to explain that I knew no one in that area so I assumed that he was looking for someone else. He smiled and said, "You may not have known anyone when you got here but you will know someone when you leave here."

He pointed to a rather nice looking woman and when she saw him pointing at her she smiled and headed our way with three children between the ages of three and six, plus a baby in her arms.

"Seaman Sullivan," he said, "meet Mrs. Norton. You are assigned to provide her assistance between here and Okinawa." I thought, *You have got to be kidding me.* She was very polite and introduced herself and told me that her husband was an Army captain stationed in Okinawa and she and the children had finally been cleared to join him there.

Things got off to a bad start. Of the three able to walk, two were girls. Of course both had to go to the bathroom. Mom looked at me with sad eyes and said, "I hate to ask you to, but you are going to have to hold the baby while I take these two to the bathroom." I had never in my life held a baby and said so. She assured me that it was no big deal and when she got me seated she handed me the baby. Thank God it was asleep. She instructed the young boy of about three years of age to sit in the seat next to me and remain there until she returned. Well she had no sooner disappeared than did the three-year-old boy. I had no idea where he had gone and I was certain that if I stood up to look for him I would drop the baby. Taking the chance of dropping the baby I stood and look around, no boy in sight. I started to go look for him and realized that if their mother came back and we were all gone she would assume abduction. Oh hell, what to do now?

Juan to the rescue! He came walking up with the little guy and being a smart ass said, "Sir, you need to keep a closer eye on your children." Everyone within earshot looked at me as if I were useless as a father. I made the little ass sit on the bench beside me and hold on to my shirt sleeve. I told him that if he let go I was going beat the living crap out of him. When his mother returned and saw everything looked normal she smiled and took the infant back. Of course now my little male problem needed to go to the bathroom. Mother looked at me and said, "Do you mind?" I felt like a pervert keeping a close eye on the little squirt, but I had lost him once and I was not going to lose him again.

Once on the plane and airborne the mother took care of the infant and I was left with the other three. It was like herding cats. The little brats were all over the plane and I was constantly getting my ass chewed by one of the crew members for not controlling them. I tried to solicit Juan's help and he just smiled and told me what a beautiful family I had. I have never had a longer flight. They just did not wear out. I prayed for them to run down and go to sleep. That happened about three hours before we landed in Okinawa and ten hours after takeoff.

****

We landed at Kadena Air Force Base late in the afternoon. I had been to Okinawa when the *Talladega* stopped there to drop off the 1500 Marines we had onboard and again on our homeward bound trip. I knew that there was some serious liberty to be had just outside the main gate—Gate 2 Street. But Juan and I were going to have to wait for a later date for that action. When we deplaned there was a Marine sergeant in the terminal and he was snatching everyone that was wearing a Marine uniform and herding us to a corner of the terminal. He knew we were coming and once he thought he had everyone that he should have, he held a muster and I was surprised when he called out Juan's and my name and indicated that we were being assigned to the Third Marine Division's Headquarters Battalion currently at Camp Hague. We were shuffled off to another sergeant who was collecting folks going to Camp Hague.

When we arrived at Camp Hague I was surprised to see not a single permanent structure on the base. The entire base was made up of Quonset huts. A Quonset hut is a lightweight prefabricated structure of corrugated galvanized steel having a semicircular cross section. The design was based on the Nissan hut developed by the British during World War I. The inside of each hut had different configurations. Some were open squad bays for berthing and some had partitioned off walls for private berthing for senior enlisted and officers. All of the berthing huts had an open area near a compartment where the "house girls" worked and stowed their belongings. There were no toilet facilities or showers in the berthing huts. If you needed to use the bathroom or take a shower there were usually two Quonsets attached end to end, positioned perpendicular and to the rear of the berthing huts.

The sergeant dropped us off at the Personnel Office where we turned in our records and orders. The personnel clerk told me that I was working in the Division Surgeon's Office. Juan went to the 3rd Med. Battalion detachment at Camp Hague.

A lance corporal led us to our respective berthing areas and then to our assigned work spaces. I found out why I was assigned to the Division Surgeon's Office—I could type. I was basically going to be clerk typist for the Division Surgeon and his staff. Juan made out a little bit better as he was going to be working in a clinic.

The senior enlisted in the Division Surgeon's Office was Senior Chief Robinson. When we met he seemed to be a nice enough guy so I thought this assignment may not be too bad. He told me to go back to my squad bay and change from my green uniform into my utility uniform.

When I got back to my squad bay there were four Okinawan women ironing uniforms in the middle of the open area. My locker was facing their work area. They were jabbering about something and my arrival did not seem to deter their conversations at all. My seabag was on my bunk, but I noticed that my bunk was made up. It was not when I first came in. Well I started to unload my seabag and hang things in my locker and place other items in my footlocker at the foot of the bed. Once I was all unpacked I knew I had to change clothes but saw no area to find any privacy. The jabbering continued and a periodic outbreak of laughter would occur.

I was aware of the openness of the sexuality of the Okinawan people, but I still was very uncomfortable undressing before an audience of women. I figured that if I started to disrobe they would excuse themselves long enough for me to change clothes. I figured wrong. I finally just said to hell with it and stripped down to my skivvies and put on my utility uniform. There seemed to be an increase in the laughter while I was dressing.

When I got back to the Division Surgeon's Office the Senior Chief asked me if the house girls were working in the common area. I said, "Yes." He laughed and said that they know how modest we Americans are and they enjoy making newcomers uncomfortable. He said that I could not have gotten them out of the common area with hand grenades. He also indicated that I would get used to it and as time went on I would not even think about it. He said, "Wait until the first time you go to take a shower and there are several house girls in the shower area washing clothes." I found out that the house girls did most of the hard work to keep us looking sharp. They hand-washed our uniforms on the floor of the showers and starched, ironed and placed our uniforms in our lockers. They polished our boots, made up our bunks every morning and changed and washed the linens twice a week.They even properly stowed our items that went into the footlockers. We paid them through the senior house girl. My monthly cost for all this labor was $12.00 plus $1.00 for the gentleman who kept the area around our hut clean and swept the sidewalk from the door to the street so often I was concerned that we would have to repave it at least every six months.

****

As the Division Surgeon's primary clerk typist my main responsibility was the typing of the daily unit diary and submitting it to the Headquarters Battalion Personnel Officer (G-1). Our diary was one of many that the G-1 compiled and forwarded to somewhere in the Hawaii Marine Corps Headquarters. Typing the diary sounds pretty simple, but absolutely no errors were permitted, no strike-overs or corrections were permitted. It had to be perfect. To make matters worse it had to be delivered to the G-1 no later than 1100 hundred each weekday. The diary recorded any event that the Division Surgeon considered important that had occurred within the past twenty-four hours and must include the names and times of all members that report for duty or are transferred. All hospitalization and incarcerations must be reported. Knowing how precise this document had to be motivated me to be in the office by 0500 each day because I knew it would take me several attempts before I got an errorless product. I also learned that a Number 11 scalpel blade could be used to remove a single typo. It had the sharpest point of all the scalpel blades and if used carefully I could actually remove a single letter and type over it without it being noticed. Of course when I got really proficient in removing a single letter mistake the assholes in G-1 learned that if they held the document up to the light and looked at it from behind they could identify such corrections. My typing skills improved significantly in the first month or so.

****

Juan and I found that we were only about twenty minutes via scosh cab (small Japanese cars) from Gate 2 Street where most of the action was. We also found out that our best friend was the Marine pay clerk that maintained our pay records. When we got paid we had to fill out a slip of paper called a pay chit. We were restricted to midnight liberty. E-6s and above had overnight liberty. An E-6 was a Navy first class petty officer or a Marine Corps staff sergeant. I never quite understood it but because of a re-structuring of the Marine Corps enlisted pay grades there were a few E-5s that were still considered as part of the top Marine Corps enlisted ranks and were given the same privileges.

There were no bunk checks so if you found yourself out and the Cinderella hour of midnight approaching you started looking for some place to hold up for the night. Then by 0900 the next morning you could freely move about again. With sufficient money you could always find an Okinawan lady to put you up. An all night stay was usually $3.00, but you could sometime get them down to $2.50.

Juan and I took good care of our pay clerk and sometimes we would draw one day's pay every day. More than once on payday we only had one day's pay on the books. As payday grew near we spent more time in the base clubs.

There were some memorable liberties in Okinawa. We made the mistake of wandering into the four corners area of Okinawa one night and found out it was the area where most of the blacks went on liberty and only blacks were welcome. Thank God the Marines believe in physical fitness. When we saw the error of our ways a group of Air Force blacks decided we would not make that mistake again. No way would they catch us as we escaped their attempt to show us that we were not welcome on their turf.

When we had the money we always headed for Gate 2 Street. One memorable night we were hitting the bars and got into an altercation with a couple of the ladies that were trying to get us to buy them drinks. The Mamasan (normally the owner or the manager) threw us out of the place. The bar was down a set of stairs off the sidewalk. As things were prone to happen, opportunity for revenge presented itself almost immediately, but it took an hour or so before we came up with the scheme. It was approaching some Okinawan holiday where they set off all sorts of fireworks. As we walked the street Juan said we should buy some firecrackers and have some fun. We bought a small arsenal for less than $2.00. They included strings of 100 firecrackers and we also bought some cherry bombs. These cherry bombs were damn near dynamite quality.

We flagged down a scosh cab and told him to circle the block. When he got to the first corner Juan lit one of the strings of firecrackers and threw it on to the sidewalk where a number of Okinawans were waiting to cross the street. Surprisingly, the pedestrians and the cab driver seemed to enjoy this event. Then the devil came out in me. We told the cab driver that we wanted to throw one of the strings down the stairs of the bar where we had earlier been ejected. It took some effort to explain what the plan was and we made two trips around the block to get the plan down pat. On the third trip we were ready. I had the window down when I realized the plan had changed. Juan took the firecrackers out of my hand and gave me one of the cherry bombs. I had to admire his creativeness. As the cab pulled near the curb Juan lit the cherry bomb and I threw it. The cab driver drove away rather quickly. But there was a problem. The cherry bomb hit the panel between the front and back seat and landed on the cab driver's headrest. Juan and I did not have time to do anything but plug our ears. When the cherry bomb went off we thought maybe we had killed the cab driver as he stomped down on the accelerator and veered across the street and plowed into several parking meters before coming to a stop. Juan grabbed my arm and we leapt out of the cab. Surprisingly, no one saw us depart and we became just part of the gathering crowd trying to understand what had happened. The poor cab driver was so stunned he could not speak or get out of the cab. We could see that there was an area about the size of a fifty cent piece where there was no hair on the back of his head. The police were on the scene quickly and Juan and I moved slowly to the back of the crowd. The last thing I remember seeing was the police trying to talk to the cab driver and he was pointing to both ears and raising his hands. The gesture at least gave us the impression that while he may never hear again he at least did not appear to have brain damage.

After that episode we decided to move our liberty somewhere else for a few months.

SEVEN

A FTER A COUPLE OF MONTHS IN THE DIVISION Surgeon's Office I had had enough being a clerk typist. I told the Chief that I wanted to go to one of the Marine battalions and that I did not want to be a clerk typist. He promised me that when the next corpsman reported with typing skills he would see to it that I got a battalion.

Luckily, within two weeks a junior corpsman reported with typing skills. Good to his word the Chief had me transferred to a Marine battalion at Camp Hansen. I was to learn that Kin Village was almost as good as Gate 2 Street as far as liberty was concerned. However, I was not there long enough to fully investigate the village. The Chief told me later that he did not know that almost as soon as I got there I would be deploying with a portion of the battalion that was going to the Philippines to participate in a joint exercise with the Australian Marines and the Philippine Army.

We landed on the island of Mindoro, the seventh largest island in the Philippines, located off the coast of Luzon near the capital city of San Juan, and established our base camp about three miles from it. The Australians were to our East, the Filipinos were to our West.

We no sooner were set up than injuries started to report to our small sickbay. We found that the Australians were anxious to prove that they were as tough as or tougher than our U.S. Marines. We shared a large tent that had been put up to serve as the enlisted club. Of course after two or three beers the challenges began and the fights, friendly as they were, could still prove quite furious. Noses were broken and teeth were knocked out. After only the first day of this exercise we knew that someone was going to have to separate the Aussies and the U.S. Marines.

One evening the crowning blow that forced the separation showed up in both our sickbay and the Aussies' sickbay. An unconscious Marine was brought to our sickbay with massive head wounds. He looked like someone had beaten him with a baseball bat. Come to find out his Aussie counterpart looked much the same. As the story unraveled it appears that the Aussies and the U.S. Marines decided to end all the fights by placing their best against each other. The decision was made that one Aussie and one U.S. Marine would stand back to back and each take five paces then turn around and place their hands behind their back and on some signal they would charge each other head first and butt heads. Both combatants took their rolls seriously and made no effort to back down. Well apparently after four such head butts they knocked each other unconscious. We had to call in a medevac for both of them and they were sent to a hospital in Manila.

****

We did a lot of people-to-people work with the locals, providing as much medical and dental care as was possible with the equipment we had. Some of these villages were in very thick jungle areas and the people wore very little in the way of clothing. The men wore something like a G-string and the women wore skirts but left their breasts bare. Most of our treatment was for minor injuries that had gone untreated and became infected. We lanced a lot of boils and cysts. The dentist pulled hundreds of teeth. We worked outdoors using any type of table we could find and had to fight the roaming pigs to keep them out of the bloody trash that we were accumulating. This was a real *National Geographic*-like adventure.

****

Several days into the exercise we were invited to play the local softball team on a Sunday afternoon. We were trucked to San Juan and had an opportunity to meet the mayor and his family. I fell in love, or maybe lust, when I saw his daughters. They were beautiful. Come to find out that the mayor's father had been a U.S. soldier who returned to Mindoro after the Second World War and married a young girl who he had fallen in love with while fighting for the local militia.

During the game my company commander, a Marine Corps captain, came and got me and said he needed to talk to me in private.

What he had to share with me was a Red Cross message saying that my father was in critical condition and that they recommended that I be sent home on emergency leave. After the initial shock I asked how I was supposed to get from where I was to Columbia, S.C., seeing as how I was on the opposite side of the world.

Travel arrangements were made pretty quickly. A small two-seat plane landed in a field near the softball game and I was told to get aboard and that I was going to Manila where I would be given transportation to Okinawa and from there to the States. Well it sounded like a good plan, but it did not work out. When I got to Manila I was told that there was no transportation to Okinawa and that I would have to fly to Hawaii and from there to the mainland. I had only my field gear and an M-14 rifle. I found a place where I could at least take a shower and shave. When I arrived in Hawaii I went to the Military Air Liaison desk and showed them my orders. As luck would have it I was not to spend a single night in Hawaii, there was a plane departing in two hours and they had room aboard for me. What shocked me was it was a civilian plane and it was headed to Los Angles!

The Military Liaison modified my orders and gave me tickets from Los Angles to Columbia. I asked, "What am I to do with this M-14 rifle?" They said they had no provisions for storing weapons so I was told to take it with me. So I boarded this civilian airliner and placed my field gear and M-14 Rifle in the overhead storage area and settled down for the flight. When we landed in Los Angles I went looking for a Military Liaison desk to try and get rid of the M-14. I could not find one and so I went looking for my departure gate. I felt kind of funny walking around the Los Angeles airport in my military utility uniform, carrying a backpack and 782 gear along with an M-14 rifle over my shoulder. No one seemed to even notice me. I found my departure gate and had to wait four hours before departure.

When I arrived in Columbia my brother-in-law, Ely, was there waiting for me. Needless to say he was somewhat shocked when he saw that I was wearing my field uniform and carrying an M-14. He took me to my parent's house where I was able to take a bath and tried to find some of my clothes that I could fit into. I was much more bulky than when I joined the Navy. The Marines had replaced my flabby body with a very fit and trim one. I weighed about fifteen pounds more, but it was all muscle.

Because I was authorized five days leave I was in no hurry to find a place to turn in my M-14. However, I was concerned with it being stolen so I asked Ely if he would take me to the Marine Corps Reserve Training Center on our way to his house where my mother and sisters were currently located. When we arrived at the training center, the staff sergeant on duty was at somewhat of a loss as to how to take custody of the M-14. He called the Marine Corps captain in charge at home for guidance. The captain told the staff sergeant to keep me there that he was on his way to the Center. When the captain arrived he seemed confused to see this guy in civilian clothing wanting to turn in an M-14 rifle. After I explained the circumstances he said no problem. He filled out a custody form and had me sign it and he signed it and gave me a copy. Rest assured I would never lose track of that custody form. I was having concerns of being charged with theft of government property.

When we arrived at my sister Fran's house I was in for another shock. My mother did not look well. I was told that she had been diagnosed with lung cancer and was starting treatment the following week. My older sister Florence and her two boys, plus my younger sister Cindy, were also at Fran's home. Fran lived in a two bedroom house with a small kitchen. The place was packed to the gills. After a lot of hugging and catching up I told them that I would be staying at Mom and Dad's house. My sister Florence and her boys would join me and my mom would stay with Fran so that she could keep an eye on her.

Later that day when I went to the hospital to visit with my dad he was obviously sick but not on his death bed. Our family physician was there and took me out into the hall to talk. He expressed his concern about not only my dad, but how he would react to the news about my mom. I knew then that I was not going to be going back to Okinawa anytime soon if I could do anything about it. Our doctor agreed that it would be best if I could stick around for a month or so to see how things were going to shake out.

With a letter from our family physician and the Red Cross, the folks at the Naval Personnel Center in Washington, D.C. agreed to place me on temporary duty at the Naval Reserve Training Center for sixty days humanitarian assignment. Fortunately, I had my Navy uniforms shipped to my mom and dad's house when I went with the Marines, so at least I had a uniform to wear.

I reported in the next day to save my leave. The Naval Reserve Training Center had no idea what to do with a hospital corpsman! I suggested that I talk to the Army hospital at Fort Jackson and see if they could employ me for the sixty days. The officer in charge (OIC) of the center was agreeable to this.

My military education was about to expand again. When I reported to the Army hospital at Fort Jackson the senior enlisted noncommissioned officer for the hospital took me to meet the Commanding Officer (CO).

When summoned to enter by the CO, I went to the front of his desk, took the position of attention and looking six inches above his head reported, "Hospitalman Hugh Sullivan reporting, Sir." He said nothing. He just sat there. I did not know what to think or do so I held my position of attention. Eventually he realized that I had gone as far as I was going to with this reporting procedure. Very loudly and aggressively he shouted, "Don't you people in the Navy salute when reporting to an officer?" I was somewhat taken aback. I very timidly responded that the Navy and Marine Corps do not salute when indoors or when uncovered unless we were under arms. He seemed amused. He asked, "Really?"

"Yes, Sir."

"Well I be damned. I have learned something new today."

I could not resist the temptation, I said, "Sir, so did I."

After a short chat about my qualifications he turned to the Senior NCO and said, "Hell, we can use him as one of our physicians if he's qualified to do all the things he claims he can do." I did not know how to take that comment. He told the senior NCO to assign me to the emergency room and let the doctors decide how qualified I was.

I found out that the average Army medic did not have near the training that I had. Between Corps School and Field Medical Service School my training was far superior to the Army medics who had only gone through their basic medic course.

Long story short, I was well received in the emergency room at the Army hospital at Fort Jackson and my two months went by very fast.

****

During my last week of the two month humanitarian assignment I was contacted by my Assignment Chief Petty Officer and he indicated that the Red Cross recommended an additional ninety days humanitarian assignment. The decision was that I would serve that assignment at the naval hospital in Beaufort, S.C. Beaufort was only a three hour drive from Columbia so I could come home on weekends.

In April of 1964 during my two months at Fort Jackson I met June— a girl who had graduated from the same high school that I had graduated from. We dated during this entire period.

When I went to Beaufort Naval Hospital the Command's Master Chief was aware of my family situation and arranged for me to stand all my after-hours duties during the week so that I could go home on the weekends. The second weekend home I married June. She moved into a trailer that belonged to my sister Fran and was parked in my parent's backyard. June did not hit it off well with any of my sisters and I wasn't sure why. I later understood their concerns. By June of '64, *my* June was pregnant.

****

During my three months at Beaufort I met and became friends with a Chinese guy who also lived in Columbia. We began to commute back and forth on the weekends together. His name was Dennis and his father was a professor at the University of South Carolina. Dennis was quite the character. We left Beaufort as early as we could on Fridays and got back before muster on Mondays. We usually bought two or three six packs of beer on Friday and drank it all on the way home. We also had an adequate amount of beer for the return trip on Sundays.

South Carolina was a "Blue Law" state and you could not purchase alcohol between midnight Saturday and midnight Sunday, unless, it was sold at a private club. We took turns buying for the return trip.

Well as luck would have it we got our wires crossed one weekend and did not have any beer for our return trip to Beaufort. On the way back, Dennis was driving and he saw a well-lighted building about one hundred feet off of the highway and decided it was a private club so we would stop and see if we could buy some beer. As it turned out it was a private club, but a black private club. Dennis said he did not care; he was going to see if he could get us some beer. Reluctantly I followed him to the door where we encountered one of the biggest black guys I had ever seen. He just stood there and waited for us to say something.

Dennis told him that we wanted to buy some beer. This bouncer suggested strongly that we were in the wrong place and we should move along. Dennis stood his ground and said, "We are not going anywhere until we get some beer." I thought, *Oh God he is going to get us killed.* Then after several exchanges and no evidence that Dennis was going to back down I noticed an older black man standing behind the bouncer. He finally stepped forward and asked where we were going. We told him to the naval hospital in Beaufort. He told the bouncer that he would take care of this and he asked us to follow him.

When we entered the club it was rocking with music and at least one hundred people dancing and drinking. The older gentleman took us to the bar and had us sit on two empty bar stools. The bartender came down and the older gentleman told him to give us two draft beers. We thanked the gentleman and asked his name. He said his name was John and that he had served in the Marine Corps and was partial to corpsmen. When we had finished our second draft beer the bartender brought us a six pack of beer in a brown bag. We offered to pay, but he said no, John was picking up the tab. As we got up to leave John stopped us and gave each of us a membership card. He said that we were welcome anytime we were in the area, but don't be bringing any buddies with you. To this day I marvel at the fact that a Chinese guy and a White guy had membership in an all-black private club.

Very quickly my three month tour at Naval Hospital Beaufort ended. And in January of 1965, to my surprise I was ordered back to the Third Marine Division in Okinawa

EIGHT

When I returned to Okinawa, the first question upon reporting was, "Where is the M-14 rifle you had with you when you left?" I produced the custody receipt and I'm sure the Marines verified that I had in fact turned the rifle in at the Reserve Center.

Starting almost immediately I wrote June at least two to three letters a week. I was concerned when she failed to write back. Eventually my letters dropped off to one a week and then one a month. None were ever answered. Throughout my entire tour of more than two-plus years in Okinawa and Vietnam I never received a letter from June. So when mail call came I always found somewhere else to be because it was painful to be the only member of my unit that never got mail.

****

Now I was assigned to the 1st Battalion, 9th Marines (1/9) at Camp Schwab. Situated on the far end of the island, Camp Schwab was home of the Marine Corps Third Division Recon. This was now February of 1965. I was promoted to third class petty officer while at Naval Hospital Beaufort. This promotion did not do much to help my assignment with 1/9. I was still a platoon corpsman.

In late March, 1/9 embarked aboard ship for transit to Vietnam. We were going to protect an Air Force base located near the city of Da Nang. Da Nang's topography is a combination of mountains and coastal plains, with high sloping mountains dominating the north and northwest. There are some ranges running into the sea. Da Nang has two seasons, the monsoon or rainy season, August-December; and the dry season, January-July. I was to find that both were miserable. In March in the Da Nang area the daytime temperatures reached up to 120 degrees with humidity in the range of 70+ percent. During the rainy season the mud in the streets can get waist deep.

During the dry season the dust was so thick that there was no avoiding it. It was in everything you ate or drank. Most of us did not wear underwear because the dust would just rub us raw.

Vietnam has every undesirable insect, animal and disease known to man. There are huge red ants, Malaria mosquitoes, bamboo fleas; and the bamboo viper, the Russell viper, pit viper and cobra. There are four inch long cockroaches and a couple of snakes that were called "Two Step Snakes" because that was all the time you had left in life if bitten by one. There were huge spiders, ugly blue lizards, rats, leeches, and flies the size of a quarter. There were centipedes longer than my finger, as well as two inch long millipedes. I don't know how many other insects there were but it had to be a huge number. There was also Malaria, Typhus, Immersion Foot, Dysentery, Heat Stroke, Tuberculosis, Leprosy, and intestinal parasites. There were some venereal diseases that are still being studied. The leeches were the most annoying, secondly were rats.

We were not allowed to smoke, use cologne, deodorant or insect repellent when not in garrison. We learned that insect repellent was the most effective way to get leeches to turn loose, but we could not use it unless in camp, where there were few leeches. Each morning when on a mission we would inspect each other for leeches. We would light cigarettes just long enough to burn them off.

All in all I would say it was a wonderful place to avoid.

****

Little did I know that we were making history. We were the first major ground unit of the U.S. Military to be assigned to Vietnam. I found out quickly that this was not going to be a fun assignment. We received mortar rounds nightly. Most landed harmlessly but sometimes the Vietcong got lucky and hit something. We received our first casualty the third day in-country. A mortar round landed near one of our defense posts and wounded three Marines. None seriously, but it brought to mind quickly that this was in fact a war zone. Daytime was a time to rest because nighttime belonged to the Vietcong.

A month or so later another Marine battalion landed in Da Nang and they were a combat battalion. We were relieved of our duties and our battalion commander decided it was time for us to do what we were trained to do, reconnaissance. We moved away from the air base a short distance, and on the first day after we had established our camp a group made its first recon patrol. They were gone for five days and returned intact with a wealth of intelligence about the local Vietcong. This information resulted in some serious aerial attacks that obviously hurt the Vietcong. Recon teams were established and rotated missions; some were as short as two days, some as long as ten.

When my team's time came to go I was a nervous wreck. I was not only concerned about running around in the enemy's backyard, but wondered if we made contact with the enemy would I do my job as trained or would I not be able to stand up to the task.

My team consisted of myself and five Marines. We were to be out five days on a mission to determine if the Vietcong were being supplied by the North Vietnamese or if they were solely living off of the local communities. We departed after dark and spent the entire night moving westward. Our team leader was a staff sergeant named Wynn.

We had made every effort to ensure that nothing on us was going to make any noise. Dog tags were taped together, all loose items on our 782 gear was secured with tape or twine. Our job was to move about without being seen or heard and collect intelligence information. As daylight approached we hunkered down near a stream bed and under some very heavy rain forest cover. We took turns staying awake, keeping an eye out for problems. I took my turn on duty right along with the Marines. I was scared, but not panicked. As dusk approached we prepared to move again. I have no idea how the staff sergeant knew where we were going or what was the best approach to our objective.

At dawn we again found a place to hunker down. Except this time we were in view of a road. Two people stayed awake and made note of anything and everything that move along the road while the remainder slept. We ate rations and buried our debris. I had the second watch of the day and it was from 1000 until 1400, a four hour watch.

Most of the movement along the road appeared to be farmers going to and from their fields and patties. At about 1300 we noticed our first vehicular traffic. There was some kind of foreign car leading four small trucks. The occupants of all five vehicles, while not wearing uniforms, were armed. We woke the staff sergeant and gave him an opportunity to observe this procession. He smiled and took out a small green book and started to take notes. To my surprise he also had a camera and took several pictures. We stayed in place another day and while I was sleeping apparently another group of vehicles containing armed military members came down the road about thirty minutes later than the day before.

Day three was uneventful and that night we started home.

We spent the fourth night near the place where we had spent the first night. On the fifth night we approached our camp but made no attempt to enter. We waited until first light and then stood tall and made our presence known by singing the Marine Corps Hymn. My first recon patrol was over and I was relieved to be back in our compound.

It did not take the Vietcong long to realize that someone was reading their mail. More and more they were the subject of attacks in their previously safe areas. They knew that our unit was separated from the air base and figured out quickly that we were the source of the information that was causing them problems. More and more we were receiving nighttime mortar rounds into our compound. However, our Marines were constantly improving our defensive posture and the mortar rounds were having little effect on us, beyond keeping us awake.

It seemed that my unit's turn to go again came quickly. This time we were going out for eight days and were going beyond the point where we had previously been. We took a radio operator and a little more ammunition and rations this time so we could not move quite as fast initially. On the fourth day out we ran into a problem. Before we could make evening camp we stumbled into a group of Vietcong who were not on a trail and were carrying weapons. A short firefight ensued. There was a gunny sergeant named Brown in charge and he directed us away from the fight. It was his plan to break off the engagement and try to move around the Vietcong and continue our mission. Well we initially were able to elude them, but they were diligent and soon found us again. They obviously had sent for additional help in rounding us up.

A second time the Gunny was successful in getting us away from the Vietcong. But with their reinforcements they again found us and we took our first casualty. One of the Marines was wounded in the hand and lost most of his thumb. I patched him up, but did not want to give him any morphine unless the pain became overwhelming. I knew he was in pain but he never complained. He informed me that he was left handed so he could still shoot his rifle. For a third time the Gunny was able to maneuver us away from the enemy. But it was obvious that we were in trouble and would not be able to avoid them forever. The Gunny finally broke radio silence and called for help. He gave our coordinates and was informed that there was a grassy area about two clicks (kilometers) from our current position and that if we could get there they would send in helicopters to extract us.

We started for the assigned area and ran headlong into about fifteen Vietcong. We had the upper hand in that we saw them before they saw us. There was no question about not fighting. We unloaded on them and the sheer surprise caused most of them to run rather than fight. The Gunny was back on the radio reporting the incident and indicating that the landing zone may be hot when the helos arrived. We got to the landing zone and the Gunny radioed that we were there and there was no sight of the enemy. They asked us to pop green smoke because there were three grassy areas in the general vicinity. We threw the smoke bomb into the center of the landing zone and almost immediately heard two helos inbound. As they began to hover we made a mad dash for them and by the time we got to them we started to receive small arms fire. The pilots never hesitated, staying in place until the last of us were aboard and then left the area as quickly as possible. To my surprise we only had the one casualty. I found out after we landed that the co-pilot in our helo had been wounded in the upper leg but he did not know it immediately. He realized that he was sitting in something wet and when he checked he saw that it was blood. I had survived another mission.

****

As spring began the remainder of the 3rd Marine Division arrived in Vietnam with the Division Headquarters being established north of Da

Nang, between Da Nang and the famous Marble Mountain. Almost every Marine had a desk nameplate made from the marble of Marble Mountain.

As the remainder of the Division arrived we continued to do our mission of reconnaissance, but more and more we were being used as the lead element in ground combat. Frequently the 1st Battalion of the Ninth Marines was pitted against some of the most determined elements of the enemy. We started to mount up some serious casualties.

Little did I know at the time but before the Vietnam War was to end, the 1st Battalion of the Ninth Marines would earn the name "The Walking Dead" for its high casualty rate. The battalion endured the longest sustained combat and suffered the highest killed-in-action (KIA) rate in Marine Corps history, especially during the Battle of July Two. The battalion was engaged in combat for forty-seven months and seven days, from 15 June 1965 to 19 October 1966 and 11 December 1966 to 14 July 1969. Based on typical battalion strength of 800 Marines and Navy hospital corpsmen, 93.63 percent (747) were Killed in Action (KIA) and 0.25 percent (2) were Missing in Action (MIA).

****

The U.S. Marine Corps launched its first major military operation known as Operation Starlite. Though the 9th Marines were not directly involved we knew something big was coming when they started to pull corpsmen from the 9th Marines to augment elements of the 3rd, 2nd, 4th Battalions of the 7th Marine Regiment. The battle was against the 1st Vietcong Regiment, which had gathered to attack the Marine Corps Air Base at Chu Lai. As the battle unfolded the ground units of the Marines were supported by U. S. Navy gunfire from offshore ships as well as UH-34D helicopters from HMM Squadrons 261 and 361. This battle included land and sea approaches.

By the end of the battle I was totally exhausted. We corpsmen found ourselves treating both U.S. Marines and Vietcong. During the entire battle I just hoped that someone in charge knew what was going on because I certainly was getting jerked here, yon and everywhere.

By the time the battle concluded we had lost forty-five Marines and had over 200 wounded. The Enemy forces sustained major casualties with well over 600 confirmed killed. There were two Medal of Honors awarded, the first of the Vietnam War.

After the battle was over I found out that I was eligible for my only out-of-country Rest and Relaxation (R&R). This was a one week period, not to be charged as leave, where we could select one of several destinations to visit and rest up. As luck would have it my friend Juan, who was also assigned to the 9th Marines, was able to also schedule his R & R with me. We decided to go to Australia. On the day before our departure we were informed that only one of us could go on R&R at this time. There was an urgent need for a corpsman with one of the platoons of Charlie Company of 1/9. We were disappointed but knew there was no need to argue. We flipped a coin and I won, so it was off to Australia for me and off to war for Juan.

When I returned to Vietnam after my R&R I got the devastating news that Juan had been killed in a running fire fight with a large and aggressive Vietcong unit. I was lost. I did not know how I would go on without my best friend. But the Marines rarely give you time to mourn. The second day back I was out on an intelligence gathering mission that lasted ten days.

NINE

I N OCTOBER OF 1965 I WAS NOTIFIED THAT I WAS BEING transferred to the 1st Marine Division at Camp Pendleton. I departed Vietnam on 1 November 1965 and flew via Okinawa to the States.

I went home to Columbia wanting a joyful reunion with my pregnant wife and my mom and dad. June acted as if nothing had changed and when questioned about her not writing she had no excuse except that she was working as a waitress at night and slept most of the day. It was obvious that my parents were in increasingly poor health. I spent five days at home during which I bought a new car. Then my wife and I started for California so I could report to the 1st Marine Division. I reported in to my new command on the 18th of November.

The wife and I settled into a small duplex and I was learning what my new job would entail.

On December 3, 1965 my company commander summoned me to his office. He had another of those dreaded Red Cross messages stating that my mother was not expected to live more than a week and requested that I be granted emergency leave. I explained to him that I did not have the money to get a plane ticket to the east coast. I had traveled across country and was flat broke. He suggested that I check with Navy/Marine Corps Relief Society to see if they would grant me a loan. I explained to him that I was hesitant to go home, because if my mom did not die and I had to return to Camp Pendleton and then she did die I would not be able to return for her funeral. He was sympathetic and understood my dilemma. Two days later another Red Cross message was received and my company commander informed me that my mom had passed away. I did not have to explain my situation, he already knew it. He told the corporal at the desk that he would be out of the office for an hour or so and for him to cover for him. He told me to follow him. He drove me over to the local commercial ticket office on the base and bought me a roundtrip ticket to Columbia. I was flabbergasted. He said, "Pay me back when you can. Now go home, get packed and get to the airport."

When I got home I explained to my wife all that had happened. I was given ten days leave and I promised her I would return as soon as possible. She was understanding and drove me to the airport.

I ran into my oldest sister's husband John in the Los Angeles airport and we talked for a few minutes. We were not on the same flight and he was to arrive about a half an hour before me, so he assured me that someone would be at the airport to pick me up.

When I got home everyone was staying in my sister Fran's home, and again I decided to stay at my mom and dad's place. I was informed that not only had my mom died, but that my dad was in the hospital. The next day I visited him and he seemed to be in good spirits. He did not question why I was home and I did not offer an explanation. We buried Mom the 8th of December, the day before her fiftieth birthday.

After the burial I went back up to the hospital and spent about four hours with my dad and again he seemed to be in good spirits. We talked about a number of things before the subject of mom came up. He asked me if she looked good for her funeral. He knew but was not going to bring it up until he knew she was buried. Even with this news and me spending another hour or so with him I left feeling pretty good about him. I went home to his house and took a good bath and settled down on the couch and fell asleep. Around 2:00 a.m. someone was knocking on my door. When I opened the door it was John and he came to inform me that the hospital had called and informed the family that my dad had passed away shortly after 11:00 p.m. two hours after I had left him.

I went through the second funeral in five days in a daze. The logistics were pretty simple in that we told the local mortuary to just do the same thing they had done for my mom. Not much time was spent on dad's funeral and we buried him the following day. The next day I headed back to Camp Pendleton.

My wife was stunned when I related the events involving my dad passing away the day we buried my mom.

I reported back to work the next day and was hit with the news that the 1st Marine Division was deploying to Okinawa as backfill for the 3rd Marine Division that was in Vietnam. I was able to get one of the airlines to allow my wife to fly even though she was eight months pregnant. Once I got her on the plane I started to consider what to do with our almost new car.

My brother-in-law, John, was stationed in Lemoore, California, and was under orders to an aircraft carrier on the east coast. I drove my car up to Lemoore and he drove it across country for me and gave it to my wife.

Two days after I returned from Lemoore we boarded ship at Long Beach Naval Station, California. Boy was I surprised to see the ship that we were going to be traveling aboard—the USS *Talladega*. I thought it would be like going home to be back aboard her. I was soon reminded that life on a troop transport is different for the troops than for ship's company.

As we were loaded aboard along with most of our rolling stock of vehicles I remembered the two Fleet Marine Force corpsmen that we had picked up on my Westpac cruise aboard the *Talladega*. Well I never got near the ship's sickbay on the trip to Okinawa. I was stuffed into a berthing compartment with 1,500 other Marines and corpsmen.

Our bunks were made from galvanized water pipes with canvas strung between the pipes. One side of the bunk was attached to the bulkhead of the ship. Or, if you were not near a bulkhead then you kind of free floated with the top bunk attached only to the overhead and two steel beams. The top bunk was attached to a cleat on the overhead and then the next bunk was attached to the top bunk and this continued to the floor. There were six bunks in each string and the distance between the rows of bunks was such that if two people met they had to turn sideways to pass each other. We had our own heads (bathrooms) and shower facilities. We were not allowed on deck except for training and limited amounts of controlled exercise. Compared to the ship's company (those actually assigned to the ship for duty) we were second-class citizens.

Once underway it seemed that every Marine in the berthing area was seasick. There was not room enough for all of them in the head and a number of them just lay on the deck in the shower areas. They took the drain covers off of the showers and periodically turned the showers on to wash the upchuck down the drains. A number of them tried to stay in their bunks, but when they got sick they could not make it to the heads or showers and before long the smell in the berthing area was outrageous. The smell contributed to others getting sick. It was a hellhole. I stayed in my bunk for the entire first two days to avoid walking through the mess. By the third day most were acclimated and most of the mess on the decks had been cleaned up.

I found that the daily routine mostly amounted to standing in line for chow. Several times I finished chow and got back in the line to await the next meal.

Shortly after we arrived in Hawaii, where we were allowed to leave the ship, but could not leave the pier, I received a Red Cross notification that my wife had given birth to a baby boy named Dee Shan Sullivan. I thought, what the hell is wrong with that woman? She has given my son a girl's name. As things tend to often go, I was to get the real story later when we arrived in Okinawa. My son was a daughter.

TEN

WE WERE IN OKINAWA ONLY A FEW WEEKS WHEN WE were informed that the 1st Marine Division was being deployed to Vietnam. I was assigned to the 2nd Battalion of the 5th Marine Regiment. 2nd Battalion 5th Marines (2/5) is an infantry battalion in the United States Marine Corps consisting of approximately 800 Marines and Sailors. It is the most highly decorated battalion in the Marine Corps and their motto, "Retreat, Hell!", comes from the French trenches of World War I, when a Marine officer named Lloyd W. Williams was ordered to retreat and he replied, "Retreat? Hell, we just got here!"

Similar to the first deployment I wrote letters frequently to June and like before I never received a response. I continued to avoid mail call.

We loaded up aboard another troop transport ship (not the *Talladega* this time) and arrived off the coast of Chu Lai, Vietnam in April 1966. The temperature was near 115 degrees when we arrived and what air conditioning there was in our berthing area was secured so that the large hatches above us could be removed to provide access to our rolling stock.

Mercifully they got us out of the below decks area as quickly as possible. Though we had fresh air on the outside decks the heat was such that the soles of our boots started to melt and stick to the ship's deck.

We made an old fashioned landing at Chu Lai by going over the side of the ship and climbing down the rope netting and into landing craft, just like it was done in WWII. This method of offloading troops is not as easy as it may appear. When you are nearing the landing craft you realize that with the motion of the ship and the landing craft you have to really time your movement from the rope netting into the landing craft because there could be as much as six to eight feet from the netting to the bottom of the craft. If you don't let loose at the right minute you could really get hurt falling six to eight feet into the landing craft. Surprisingly, with no prior experience we did not have a single serious injury loading our craft.

We did not know what to expect when we landed on the beach. Was this going to be one of those WWII landings where we had to fight our way off of the beach? We had all been issued live ammunition so we assumed there was at least the possibility that we would encounter hostiles when we arrived. We were pleasantly surprised when the front ramp of our landing craft dropped down and we were met by a rather large group of Vietnamese kids trying to sell us trinkets and water.

****

I was abducted, that is the only way I can explain it, by a Marine Corps captain and told that I was his driver and that we were going to lead convoys inland to the site where the Division Headquarters would be established. There was no argument to this order and I drove his jeep back and forth from the beach to the HQ area at least ten times going deep into the night.

Finally, on one of our trips he said, "Doc, it is time for me and you to get something to eat and a hot cup of coffee." He gave me directions to a hastily established chow hall where the Marines were fixing breakfast for the arriving troops. Never has coffee tasted so good. We had a plate of reconstituted eggs and bacon which tasted like a gourmet meal. After eating he finally asked me what unit I was assigned to. When I told him 2/5 he said, "Hell, they are setting up ten miles from here. Oh well, we'll get you there somehow or another." Later in the morning he came back to the chow hall and got me and said that he had found a group that was going to 2/5 and I was to go with them. He thanked me for driving all night and wished me luck. He said, "One final thought: you are going into Indian country, so keep your head down."

Upon arriving at 2/5 I was directed to Charlie Company where I met with the first sergeant, a very familiar master sergeant. My old friend Gunny Henderson from Field Medical Service School was now the first sergeant of Charlie Company. The senior enlisted member of a company is referred to as the first sergeant, regardless of his actual rank. He grinned and asked, "Do you do still want to kick my ass?" I smiled and said, "No,

I'm looking for a Gunny Sergeant Henderson." He laughed and asked if I was still running the beaches in my combat boots. I smiled back and said, "No, First Sergeant. I'm now running the jungles of Vietnam with full 782 gear, body armor, and a seventy pound backpack."

He asked where I had been since he last saw me and I filled him in on my tour with the 3rd Division and the loss of my parents. He asked about my Mexican buddy, Juan. I choked up as I told him that Juan was no longer with us. I asked about Captain Leggett and again the first sergeant smiled and said, "Oh I think you will see him around the area from time to time." I soon found out that Captain Leggett was now Major Leggett and was the company's CO.

The first sergeant told me that he would like to keep me there in Charlie Company Headquarters, but that all the rifle companies were short of platoon level corpsmen. I was a third class corpsman so that meant that I would probably be assigned to a squad in one of the platoons.

I was assigned to one of three rifle platoons in Charlie Company; each platoon had four corpsmen assigned. There was a senior corpsman assigned to the Platoon Leaders Headquarters.

****

There is no description that can fully enable someone that has not experienced combat to understand the emotions one experiences when going face-to-face with a determined enemy trying to kill you. We spent a lot of our time looking for trouble and frequently found it. Sometimes very short but vicious experiences and sometime prolonged engagements where the enemy was trying to extract as much pain as possible without having an all-out, face-to-face confrontation. Unfortunately people are killed and injured in both circumstances.

Within a span of one month, Alpha Company lost two of their corpsmen and Charlie Company lost two of our corpsmen. In the case of Alpha Company, they also lost their CO.

****

The monsoon season was upon us and I don't believe anyone who has not experienced the monsoon season in Vietnam can appreciate rain in the proportions that it occurs. The rain drops were the size of a quarter and it frequently rained sideways. Within ten days of the first rains the company streets were knee deep in mud. It was such a chore that we started to take turns going to chow. As before with the 3rd Division, three people would wade through the mud to the chow hall and eat. Then they would fill their trays with as much food as they would hold, place a borrowed rain parka over the trays and wade back to the tent to feed the men that had not gone. The next meal, three other men would make the trip. This was a familiar exercise. It was hard to believe that the dust that we had in everything we wore or ate was now mud two to three feet deep. Going on operations in this mess was a real adventure. Mostly the Vietcong and the NVA preferred to not fight during the monsoon season, but to the extent that we could find them we made them fight.

On one of our platoon-size sweeps we went into an area where a unit of the NVA had been reportedly sighted. We were planning to be out for about ten days. I chose to continue to carry my M-14 rifle where as several of the other platoon corpsmen were now armed with WWII 12-gauge shotguns. During this outing we spent a lot of time crossing flooded rice patties. These patties were overflowing because it was the monsoons. Even when we were not in rice patties we were in mud up to our ankles and never dry. We tried to sleep when the opportunity presented itself but it was a miserable half sleep. We spent a great deal of our time inspecting each other for leeches.

Unlike 1/9 where we were trying to avoid being found, with 2/5 we were looking for a fight and did not care if the enemy knew we were there. So, the best thing to use to get the leeches to release their blood sucking hold on you was to squirt our insect repellent on them. We smelled at times like a walking bug spray factory. The leeches were the one thing that bothered me the most. You rarely knew they were attached to you until someone found them. Leeches aside, on this operation I developed a bad case of emersion foot, or jungle rot as it was frequently called. I knew my left foot was a problem, but I was not about to take my boot off for fear of not being able to get it back on. I started to run a fever.

By the sixth day of the operation my temperature was hanging steady at 102 degrees. My squad leader noticed that I was not doing well and asked what was going on. I told him that I had an infection in my left foot but did not know how bad it was yet. By day eight I was in trouble. My temperature was up to 104 degrees and there was a red line running from my foot to my groin. I did not want to be the cause of the mission being aborted, but I knew that something had to be done. The platoon staff sergeant finally informed the platoon commander that they needed to medevac me out or I might lose a foot. After a short conversation with him he called for a medevac and shortly I was on my way back to the medical battalion supporting the 5th Marines.

When I was taken off of the helicopter and the doctors cut my boot off, one of them actually threw up at the sight of my foot. I was immediately evacuated to the naval hospital in Da Nang.

There were always reporters there asking questions and taking pictures when a medical evacuation plane landed at Da Nang. While I was a litter case I was almost embarrassed to have my picture taken along with the truly wounded Marines that were also being evacuated with me.

When I got to the hospital two doctors examined at my left foot and both came to the quick conclusion that my left big toe and the second toe needed to be removed. I listened with concern and finally asked, "Isn't there any way to save my toes?" They discussed it a little further and came to the same conclusion, the toes must go. I asked who their boss was and they said Commander Ryan. I said that before I could consent to any surgery I wanted to talk to him. They seemed a little put off by my request, but said they would inform him. About two hours later Commander Ryan and the two knuckleheads were back looking at my foot. To my surprise Commander Ryan said that he thought there was a possibility that my toes could be saved, but there was also a possibility that I could develop gangrene and lose my entire foot. He said it was my call, but he was willing to give a shot at saving the toes. I said that I was willing to take the risk. I could tell that the two knucklehead doctors were hoping for gangrene.

After five days of treatment the saving of my toes was beginning to look promising. New tissue was growing and the partial toenail on the big toe was starting to grow. The toenail on the second toe was not going to regenerate. Within ten days it was obvious that I was not going to lose either of my toes. If I had known then that later in life I would require five more surgeries on my big toe, I may have made a different decision. The treatment for my toes was soaking them in Epson salt twice a day.

I met an Army medic who was in the bed beside me and we hit it off. He was being treated for a wound in the side of his neck that was pretty ugly, but not life threatening. He was assigned to an Army Special Forces team that worked out of a safe house in Da Nang. We decided to ask the attending physician if it was absolutely necessary for us to occupy a bed when we were only receiving treatment twice a day. The doctor agreed to allow us to have liberty and stay in the safe house at nights if we would be there in the morning and again in the afternoon for our treatments. I was in for an interesting week with the Army Special Forces.

When we first entered the safe house, my new friend, Philip, took me to meet with the senior enlisted member of the ten-man team. The senior enlisted member agreed to allow me to stay over until my treatment was finished. As it turned out the OIC was a guy from my home town of Columbia, S.C. I did not know him but as we talked we knew some common people, mostly athletes from the Columbia area.

The Special Forces team mostly sat around and played pinochle. Most evenings, "ladies of the night" were allowed for any of the team members that were so inclined.

One night I heard small arms fire outside and near the safe house. No one seemed to hear it or at least they were ignoring it. Eventually the Army captain in charge had enough and slammed his fist down on the table and reached under the table and came out with a grease gun and started to the door cursing. I looked at Philip and he just shrugged his shoulders. Shortly I heard the captain's grease gun on what sounded like full automatic. After a few seconds all was quite outside. Philip smiled and said this happens about once a week. I asked, "What happens?" He said that there was an Army nurse compound across the street and their guard and ours did not like each other and periodically they started shooting at each other. Neither was trying to hit the other, just put pot holes in each other's cement guard shack. He said that the captain would only tolerate this for a few minutes and then would shoot up the exterior of the nurse's guard shack and everything would go quite after that.

I was amazed that they seemed to have all the booze they wanted. But I also learned that at least twenty-four hours before a mission those deploying quit drinking.

One such mission occurred while I was staying at the safe house. I noticed that a sergeant and a staff sergeant were not drinking one evening and the next evening some strange looking characters started to appear in the safe house, all Oriental. I asked Philip if he could tell me what was going on. He said all he could say was that a mission was going down tonight and the two Americans and eight of the mercenaries would be leaving soon for a helo lift out. He pointed to a couple of the mercenaries and said that he had operated with them on several occasions and they were fearless and mean as hell--unbelievable operators.

****

All good things must come to an end and after five days in the safe house and going to the hospital twice daily for treatment I was discharged to light duty. I was to go somewhere that I could continue my treatment for another two weeks. That somewhere was the 1st Division Headquarters.

Thankfully the monsoon season was coming to an end.

When I reported to the 1st Marine Division Headquarters, the first sergeant assigned me to "Graves Registration," the worst job in the military. The job entailed receiving bodies from the front lines and, to the extent that we could, identifying them. We then had to tie off their penis and stuff gauze into every orifice in the body—including the nose, ears, mouth and anus. Sometimes when we opened a body bag it would just contain body parts and at times it was obvious that the parts were not all from one individual. When we received a body that was pretty much intact the body could almost always tell a story. I remember one staff sergeant that had a minor wound in the shoulder and it had been treated and bandaged by someone. His coloring was different. At first I thought that maybe he had died of shock, but further examination showed a small caliber wound in his chest that was not obvious when I first examined him. He obviously had been wounded and left for medevac when one of the enemy soldiers came across him and shot him point blank in the chest.

As luck would have it, the 1st Marine Division Surgeon's Office learned that I was over at Graves Registration but really should have been at the Division Surgeon's Office. So they arranged to have me reassigned. I tried to hide my typing skills, but it was soon discovered by reviewing my service record that I could type. At least they had a typist already doing the unit diary. I was used mostly for typing letters. For almost a month I continued my twice daily treatments on my toes and they healed up nicely.

****

One of my duties while at the Division Headquarters was to accompany an ensign to make the pay rounds at the end of each month. This entailed us going to all of the 1st Marine Division Battalions and paying all medical, dental and chaplain personnel. No one was allowed to have U.S. greenbacks so the pay was in "Military Pay Script." On one of our pay runs I was driving the jeep and we came to what had previously been a small stream. However, the Monsoons were beginning and the stream was wider than it had been on previous trips. The ensign decided that it was still shallow enough to cross. About ten feet from the bank the jeep started to float. Before we realized it the pay boxes were floating out of the jeep and heading down stream. The stream flow eventually pushed the jeep near enough to the forward bank that we were able to get out of the stream. I will never forget the ensign looking at me and saying, "Oh shit, there goes over $300,000 and my career down the stream." We made an effort to catch the pay boxes but were not successful. I figured that I was safe but that the ensign was probably headed for prison. Fortunately for us there was a high spot downstream that caught the boxes and a Marine patrol spotted them and brought them into their headquarters. When we arrived we were very relieved to find that our payroll was intact.

****

One day, as I waited at the front bunker to the compound, I noticed a young Vietnamese boy, age six or seven, who was staring at me. I motioned him over and gave him a pack of chewing gum. We were instant buddies. When the jeep came to pick me up to go retrieve the laundry my young friend jumped into the back and motioned for us to go. We looked at each other and said "What the heck." When we got back to the forward bunker my little friend motioned that he wanted to join us in the compound. We did not know if this was permissible or not but decided if it was a problem someone in authority would let us know.

He was the cutest little guy we had ever met. We nicknamed him "Short Round." He was an instant hit with all the guys in the tent. But he seemed to be my best buddy. Everywhere I went he was right beside me. If I saluted an officer he would also salute; the officers returned his salute with a smile.

As it began to get late I walked him back to the forward bunker and he saluted me and indicated that he would be back tomorrow.

The next day, just out of curiosity, I walked down to the forward bunker and there he was waiting for me. My tent mates and I decided that if he was going to be with us he was going to need to be cleaned up and get some better clothes. We found a large tub and put him in and gave him a good bath. We washed his clothes and hung them up to dry. We gave him a towel to wrap around himself while we waited for his clothes to dry. I noticed one of the Marines was trying to measure his waist and leg length with a piece of string, then his arm length and chest size. I asked what he was doing and he said that he was going to mail the strings home and ask his mom to try and buy some clothes for Short Round. About two weeks later the clothes arrived with a couple of boxes full of toys. It was not quite Christmas but we decided to celebrate something. His new clothes fit fairly well, though they were sufficiently large enough to allow some growth.

We were surprised at how the camp was accepting Short Round and how little hassle we were receiving. However, the Division sergeant major came to me and said that the mess tent was off limits to Short Round. I said no problem and at chow time we just made him a tray of food and he ate in our tent.

When I took him to the forward bunker one afternoon he was all dressed up in his new clothes and had an arm full of toys. I watched as he paraded down the street with his goodies and was shocked when all of a sudden several older boys pounced on Short Round and took all of his toys away from him. I shouted for them to stop and the Marines manning the bunker threatened to shoot them if they did not give him his toys back. The older boys just laughed and took off running with their stolen goods. Short Round stood up and brushed himself off and looked at me. I was so mad I could not see straight. Short Round stood as straight and stiff as he could and gave me a perfect salute, did an about face and marched down the street. I thought, my God what character this young man has. If he survived this war I felt that he had a bright future.

****

During this brief stay at the Division Surgeon's Office I learned to hate something almost or perhaps more than the leech. Vietnam has the largest and most aggressive rats of anywhere in the world. They ran freely throughout our compound. One of my tent mates wrote home and requested that twenty-four rat traps be sent to him. Rat traps, not mice traps. When they arrived we were all excited to start reducing the rat population of our compound.

The first night we had the rat traps we set all twenty-four of them and as the sun set we waited and counted as we heard them go off. After the last one went off we called it a night and could hardly sleep wanting to see what we had caught the following morning. Boy, were we surprised! We had actually killed two rats; the remainder of the traps were empty and three were missing. We assumed that the three missing ones were just carried off by the rat that had tripped the trap. The following night we staked the traps to the ground or tied them to something we figured the rats could not haul off. We fared a little better the next morning in that we had actually trapped seven rats. Only one was dead so we had to physically kill the remainder.

The rat story got only worse before I transferred out. I found that a female rat had gnawed through the back of my footlocker and had built a nest in among my clothes. There were about a dozen baby rats in my footlocker. I had had enough and was not satisfied with killing them, I wanted to torture them. I went to the mess hall and got an empty twenty-pound coffee can and stopped by the water buffalos (a large water tank on a trailer that was the source of most of our drinking water) and filled the can half full of water. When I returned to my tent I captured all the babies and dropped them into the can of water. Though their eyes were not open they could still swim. I took my K-Bar knife and pushed their heads under the water but they continued to surface and swim around the can of water.

Enough! I went in to the tent and got my cigarette lighter fluid and squirted it on to the surface of the water and then lit the fluid. The rats would dive under the water to avoid the fire and then come back up for air. I was in the process of trying to keep them under the water with my K-Bar knife when I noticed someone behind me. I looked up and it was the Division chaplain. He was shocked at what I was doing and ordered me to immediately cease and desist. I told him to go somewhere else if he did not like me killing rats. He left and I eventually successfully killed all the little bastards. Later I was informed that I had been placed on the report (charged with a crime) by the chaplain. The Division Surgeon was delighted. He said that I had made history. No one has ever been placed on the report by a chaplain. As amusing as he thought it was, the Division Surgeon decided that it was time for me to go back to my unit as my foot was sufficiently healed to perform regular duty. I never heard anything else about the report chit, so I guess someone talked the chaplain out of making an issue of the event.

It was time to go back to my battalion. I said my goodbyes to Short Round and he gave me a hug that will be in my memories the rest of my life.

****

I shipped back to 2/5 and stayed at the Battalion Aid Station for a couple of days before being reassigned to a platoon in Alpha Company.

ELEVEN

I HAD FOUR MORE MONTHS TO GO ON MY CURRENT tour and I was wasting away to nothing. I had lost forty-nine pounds in the first eight months of this tour. I never had a normal bowel movement. My stomach ached constantly. No matter what or how much I ate I could not gain weight.

I met a Marine staff sergeant with the same name as mine except his middle initial was different. He was about four years older than me and referred to me as his "little brother." He was a selectee for gunny sergeant, but before he was promoted he was selected to warrant officer, and then was promoted to 2nd lieutenant (2d Lt.). All of these promotions came within two months. When he was promoted to 2d Lt. he was transferred out to be a platoon leader. Within three months of his transfer I heard that he had been killed in a night mortar attack.

I once again found myself with a rifle platoon in Alpha Company.

The second night I was there we were hit pretty hard with mortar fire and shortly after it started there was a shout that the enemy was in the compound. I was as deep in my slit trench of a foxhole as I could get. But it was obvious that this was not a normal harassment mortar attack, but something bigger. There was rifle fire all around me and mortars still coming in. The whole thing lasted no more than twenty minutes, but seemed like twenty hours.

As the shooting ceased and I heard Americans communicating I got brave and came out of my hole. I was stunned to see dead Vietcong all over the place. There must have been close to twenty within thirty yards of where I stood. Suddenly I heard a Marine call, "Doc, get over here we have a wounded Vietcong that needs assistance." When I arrived I could see that the wound, while serious, was not life threatening. He had lost the heel of his left foot. I knelt down and laid my rifle beside him. As I started to work on him, all of a sudden he grabbed my rifle up near the front sites. Instantly I grabbed the rifle at the trigger area and it went off. I did not realize what had happened at first. A Marine standing next to me said, "Damn Doc, did you have to do that?" The round that fired went through the Vietcong's chin and came out the back of his head. I was stunned! I knew right then that this was one of those events that would be with me for the rest of my life.

****

One night, about a month after the incident with the Vietcong, we started to take some mortar rounds while in garrison, which was not uncommon. We all headed to our areas of protection with the plan to sit this one out. Well, all of sudden much larger rounds started to land within the compound. One of the first two or three landed close enough to me that it blew me up into the air. I received no wounds other than I lost all hearing. After the attack was over I went to the Battalion Aid Station and was told that both eardrums were busted. Blood was flowing out of both ears. The doctor decided to keep me at the Aid Station for a few days just to see how serious the problem was. Within three days my hearing started to return. Within two weeks I could pretty much hear as normal. The doctor said that upon examination the eardrums were healing. So back I went to my platoon.

****

Life with the Marines is in no way like life with the Navy. I grew to love my Marines and they treated me with the greatest of respect. They knew that when they needed me I would be there for them. And I never used my position as a corpsman as an excuse to ride in the jeep with the officers when everyone else was marching. They respected the corpsmen who lived with them and did not complain. Oh, we all complained, but that is normal for foot soldiers. There was always a little fun joking about me being a sailor but it was never malicious.

The next four months were typical in that we took our turn doing sweeps. I was always happy when we returned from an uneventful sweep and no one was hurt or killed. Unfortunately, not all outings were uneventful. When the crap hit the fan the senior enlisted would always make sure I was as near him as possible. Not because he was concerned about himself, but because he was concerned about me. The Marines took great effort to ensure my safety because they knew that if needed, I was no good to them if I were out of action myself. I don't recall ever taking any unnecessary risk, but when a Marine was injured, if the other Marines could not get him to me I went to him. The fact that the Marine I was trying to help was wounded right where I was going was always in the back of my mind. I don't ever recall not responding to a call for, "Corpsman up!"

When you couple the misery of living in such a hostile climate with the combat and the fact that I had not had a normal bowel movement in over a year there is no description for this. When I crapped it was just a stream of water. However, I noticed that most of us were suffering from the same problem so I did not try to figure it out. I decided that if I survived and went home and my routine and food became normal, things would return to normal.

****

I went to Vietnam the first time as a 3rd class corpsman and at the end of my second tour I was a 1st class corpsman. I had earned two field promotions.

TWELVE

WHEN MY TOUR WAS UP I ROTATED BACK THROUGH Okinawa to retrieve my uniforms and other personal gear that had been stored there when we deployed to Vietnam.

I remember the day that we took our footlockers to the massive warehouse and stored them by units. The warehouse was almost full of foot lockers when we deployed. When I went to retrieve my belongings I was stunned with how few footlockers were currently in the warehouse. I'm sure some were removed for the same reason that I was retrieving mine, their tours were up. However, I was equally sure that a lot them were shipped home to surviving family members.

I was being transferred to a Marine Corps transient unit in Hawaii until I could get orders to my next duty station. When I arrived in Hawaii I had a message to call my detailer. I called the West Coast detailer and he informed me that my sea duty was not up but that he was dropping me to the East Coast detailer so as to ensure that I did not make it back to Vietnam for a third tour. I thanked him profusely!

Sea tours were determined by the availability of shore billets. It was called seavay/shorevay. Depending upon your rating some sea tours were much longer than others. We were going through corpsmen at a rapid rate in Vietnam so our tours were longer than say a personnelman's. When I got through to the East Coast detailer he informed me that I was to be assigned to the USS *Howard W. Gilmore* (AS-16), a submarine tender homeported in Charleston, S.C.

Since I had not heard from my wife in almost a year I had no idea how to contact her. When I arrived in Los Angeles I called my sister Fran and asked her if she had any idea where my wife was living. Fran said that she thought she knew, but asked me to come to her house and we'd talk about it. She sent Ely out to the airport to meet me and he was nice enough, but he was not willing to discuss the whereabouts of my wife with me. He simply said he did not know. When we arrived at my sister's house she had the coffee on and suggested that I stay with them for a few days. She asked with concern, "How much weight have you lost?" I replied, "Almost fifty pounds." She did not say anything else but I could see concern in her eyes.

I asked her if she knew what was going on with my wife, and she said that she hated to be the one to break the news to me, but that she had seen my wife with several different men during the past year and that she was working as a waitress in a local restaurant. I asked her if she knew where she was living. She said yes and told me the address. It was a home outside of the main gate at Fort Jackson, S.C. I told her I wanted to get cleaned up and see if I could get in touch with her. She was concerned about me and what would happen when I went to her home.

Around 5:00 p.m. I found the address that my sister had provided and knocked on the door. A young woman answered the door. I asked, "Does June Sullivan live here?"

"Yes but she's not home, she's at work," she said.

"Where is her daughter. Dee?"

"Here. I'm babysitting her."

I asked if I could see her. She refused and closed the door in my face. I thought I heard a man laughing inside the house, but could not be sure. I went back to my sister's car and found pencil and paper and wrote June a note letting her know that I was home and staying with Fran. I asked her to give me a call.

It was a little after 10:00 p.m. when June called and with surprise in her voice she said that she did not know I was coming home. I said, "If you had read any of my letters you would know." This bit her but she remained calm and asked where I was headed for duty. I told her that I was going to a ship homeported in Charleston, S.C. She said that she had tomorrow off and wanted to know if we could get together for breakfast the next day. I told her that I would pick her up around 8:00 in the morning.

When I got to her house she came out and got into the car. She did not have Dee with her. I asked why she did not bring Dee and she stated that she was still sleeping and thought we could better talk without her along.

She also asked how much weight I had lost and when I told her almost fifty pounds she asked why I wanted to lose weight. I told her it was not intentional, but the environment that I had lived in for the past two years was not the healthiest of places and the food was nothing to write home about.

We went to a local diner and I do not remember what I had to eat, because I was so nervous. After a few tense minutes she asked if she and Dee were invited to join me in Charleston. At first I was hesitant to respond, but I wanted so much to have a family and live with my daughter and wife that I said I was hoping that she wanted to. She looked at me like I was crazy and said, "Of course we want to. When are we leaving?" I told her that I was authorized thirty days leave and had ten days travel and proceed time. Proceed time is normally three days of free leave associated with a permanent change of station orders. Travel time is computed on distance and mode of travel. I told her I would like to leave as soon as she could so we could obtain housing and get settled before I had to check into the ship.

She still had the car that we had owned in California and it appeared to be in good condition. I took the car and had my brother-in-law ride back over to get his car.

While I was back at home in the land of the big PX, I found that I was having trouble eating. Shortly after eating I would get acid indigestion and stomach cramps. So I ate very little and what I did eat was absolutely absent of any spices.

Two days later I came to her house and met my daughter Dee for the first time. She was beautiful. I had my stuff in the car and it did not take much time to load June's and Dee's belongings into the car. Off we went to Charleston.

We spent the first night in North Charleston in a motel and were at the housing office on the base when it opened. To my surprise they looked at my orders and told us that they had civilian owned, government contract housing and there were several units available. The homes were pretty much the same so we didn't even go out to look at our new home we just took the keys to one of the units and with the address we went out to look. The house was actually located in Goose Creek, S.C. which was about twenty miles from where the ship was located. The house was furnished with government furniture so all we had to do was place our belongings where we wanted them and go do some grocery shopping and buy a few other things such as a shower curtain.

Our first night together as man and wife since I had deployed to Vietnam was wonderful. If I was to believe what my sister Fran had shared with me June had had plenty of practice while I was gone.

The next morning I got up and Dee was awake and she let me pick her up and take her into the living room. I got my first experience at changing a diaper. It was not a work of art, but I got her cleaned up and after a fashion had a fresh diaper on her. I took her to the kitchen and placed her in her highchair and decided to make a pot of grits for me and her. To my surprise she loved them. Also to my surprise grits was one thing that didn't seem to upset my stomach. June awoke about an hour and a half after Dee and I had been up. She seemed pleasantly surprised that I had changed Dee's diaper and had fed her. She said my guess on what to give Dee was a good one because grits was her favorite. Way to go Dad!

That day I went to the store and bought a "Radio Wagon" with wooden sides. Every day I would pull Dee around the neighborhood and she really enjoyed it. The routine of me getting up first and changing and feeding Dee took hold and when I was home that was my responsibility, one that I actually looked forward to.

I took another week with my new family before I decided to report to work. I should have taken two weeks.

****

I reported to the USS *Howard W. Gilmore* (AS-16) and when I got to sickbay I found things much the same as they had been on the *Talladega*, except the amenities such as the geedunk and the chowhall were like a luxury liner compared to the Talladega. All the corpsmen but one slept in sickbay, though they had berthing elsewhere in the ship. The one that chose not to sleep in sickbay was obviously gay, so I guess he did not fit in. As luck would have it there was a senior chief petty officer who was the senior enlisted member of sickbay and a chief petty officer who was our pharmacy petty officer, and the senior chief's second in charge.

I found myself standing duty much the same as was the case on the *Talladega*. Port and starboard at sea, and four section when in port. The bad news was that I reported in on a Friday after lunch only to find out that the ship was deploying on Monday. So I spent Saturday and almost all day Sunday moving my gear aboard and getting settled.

I thought of the conversation with my detailer when he told me I was going to a ship that rarely ever deployed. He really was telling me the truth. The *Gilmore* was going to the Caribbean to undergo an Operational Readiness Inspection (ORI) and to participate in an annual war game called "Operation Springboard."

This was June's second experience with me leaving her and Dee while I went off to do the Navy's bidding. She asked if it would upset me if she took Dee and went back to Columbia and stayed with her mother while I was gone. The deployment was for ninety days and I could understand her not wanting to be alone for that long a period. So I raised no objections.

We departed Charleston on Monday morning and were at sea for about ten to twelve days during which time we exercised a number of drills that were part of our ORI.

We entered the port of San Juan, Puerto Rico, and tied up at the commercial piers. The Naval Station San Juan was about two miles from where we were tied up. There was a British aircraft carrier also anchored out near where we were tied up. My experience with the Australian Marines came to mind and I wondered if the Brit's were as crazy. To my surprise the Brits may have been even crazier. But they seemed to be happy proving that they could drink more than their American brothers.

I noticed that alcohol consumption seemed to keep my stomach from acting up and hurting, but over consumption caused great problems. It was at about this time that I started to notice blood in my stool. Not much, but enough for me to be concerned. The doctors on the ship decided that I had a stomach ulcer. I was living on antacid tablets and Alka-Seltzer.

****

As it always seems, the more rank one obtains the more rank is required to get the special privileges. First class and below had Cinderella liberty and had to be back on the ship by midnight. Chief petty officers and above could stay out all night.

The Navy was changing, but kind of slowly then. We underwent a rather rigid personnel inspection before we were allowed to leave the ship. Like the *Talladega* we had to be spotless to depart, but they didn't care what we looked like when we returned.

I learned lessons during my shipboard duties that served me well later in life.

On my first liberty in San Juan I was waiting to leave the ship when I heard a commotion on the pier and I could not believe what I saw. There were a number of local kids hawking almost everything including their sisters. There were several offering shoe shines. One kid was offering one of the Sailors a shoe shine and the sailor got a little heavy handed with the kid and the next thing everyone knew the kid opened a bottle of black liquid shoe polish and threw it all over the sailor's nice clean white uniform. I think that the only thing that saved the kid was the sailor was so stunned that it took a minute or two for him to react. By then the kid was long gone. Lesson learned; don't mess with the locals unless it is in a positive way.

****

I had made a new friend, Rodney Parish; we spent a lot of time together on the ship and went on our first liberty together in San Juan. We caught a bus to the downtown area and while some of the area was old and historic some was relatively new. The old part of the city had one main street. I found it interesting that one side of the main street was "off limits" but the other side was okay. Later that afternoon we made our way to the Acey Deucey Club on the naval base. The Acey Deucey Club restricted entrance to military in the pay grades of E-5 and E-6. Or, in the Navy's case, first class and second class petty officers. The place was rocking. We found a table with two empty seats and asked if we could join them. We were welcomed.

Rodney and I had a lot of catching up to do as far as drinking was concerned. There were probably ten guys at our table and about half were British sailors. I got my first chance to see just how crazy these Brits were when I went to the head for the first time. The head had one long stainless steel urinal with water running down the backside and was sloped so that the urine and water ran out of a drain at the left end of the urinal. Lying in the urinal on his back with his arms folded across his chest was a British sailor. Well, I thought, that was strange, but even stranger were two British sailors peeing on their shipmate and appearing not to even notice that he was in the urinal. I did not have the heart to follow their example so I used one of the toilets in one of the stalls. Rodney and I decided that if we stayed in the club we were sure to get into trouble. We returned to the ship.

Upon arrival at the ship we noticed some commotion around one of the conveyer belts going into the ship. The ship was loading stores (supplies) and the commotion surrounded two Sailors that were too drunk to climb the after brow, so the Sailors loading stores were in the process of placing the drunks on the conveyer belt and delivering them into the ship's chow hall.

****

When we left Puerto Rico we made a two day, one night stop at St. Thomas in the U.S. Virgin Islands. This was the highlight of the cruise as far as I was concerned. There were somewhere between six and eight U.S. ships in St. Thomas with us. Our ships could not tie up to the seawall so we had to anchor out and run liberty boats back and forth. The liberty boats made stops at each ship and loaded Sailors going ashore until the boat was full. The same process worked bringing Sailors back.

Liberty was over for all hands at 2300 the first and only night that we were there. Rodney and I did a little shopping and had a few drinks and before we knew it, it was time to head back. We arrived at the landing around 2230 and there was a sizable number of Sailors waiting in line for the liberty boats.

There was a commotion with one of the captain's gigs and we decided to see what was going on. Well, one rather big and completely drunk second class petty officer had decided he was not going back to the ship on a liberty boat, but would go first class with one of the COs. The Shore Patrol officer and five enlisted Shore Patrol members were studying the situation when the officer ordered two of the five to physically remove the sailor from the captain's gig. As soon as the first one grabbed the drunken sailor's arm the fight broke out and one of the Shore Patrol was tossed over the side. The officer sent the other three to assist the one that was getting beaten pretty badly. Between the four they eventually subdued the drunk, but he put a few knots on their heads before they were able to handcuff him.

We thought that was amusing but were not prepared for what took place next. We got on our liberty boat and when we were about fifty yards from shore a sailor stood up and dove over the side of the boat. I thought the helmsman was going to have a heart attack. With the help of his assistant they finally got the idiot back into the boat. No sooner had the boat gotten underway that two more idiots jumped over the side. The helmsman was beside himself. He got on his radio to report what was going on and requested assistance. While awaiting assistance three more bailed out. By the time two other liberty boats arrived there were a half dozen Sailors in the water raising hell. It must have taken an hour and a half to get everyone into the boats and off-loaded at their respective ships. I thought I would piss my pants I was laughing so hard.

****

From St. Thomas we headed for home. But the excitement of the cruise was not over. We made a two day stop at Fort Lauderdale, Florida. The word passed that only chief petty officers and above would be allowed to remain out overnight. We junior enlisted were required to be back by midnight.

Rodney and I decided to stay near the port and drink then we could drink a little longer than if we went downtown. We went into a restaurant that had a small bar just outside of the dining room. We decided to eat in the bar area and ordered hamburgers and fries with our beer. We had just finished our meal when an older couple came into the bar. It was obvious that the waiter knew them because he brought them their drink before they were even able to order. When they saw us they asked the waiter to invite us to join them. We were a little curious, but figured that maybe we could con them out of a beer. No conning necessary; the waiter had already been instructed to bring us a beer. We introduced ourselves and because it was still early we were still sober. The gentleman asked which ship we were aboard and we told him the *Gilmore*. He said that he was retired from the Navy and while enjoying retirement, he missed the Navy. We made small talk for about forty-five minutes and then he and his wife got up and were preparing to leave. Before he left he asked us if we enjoyed fishing. We of course said we did. He said that he was going out tomorrow morning around 0900 and invited us to join him. We accepted his offer. They left and we commenced to do some serious drinking.

We asked the waiter to keep an eye on the time and to run us out by 2230. Good to his word, at 2230 he told us he could not serve us anything else and we needed to get back to the ship. Rodney and I both were in pretty bad shape when we got to the ship, but we got back on time and decided to sleep in sickbay.

Somewhere in the early morning fog of our brains Rodney woke me up and said that he and I were being summoned to the quarterdeck. I sat on the edge of my bunk determined to hear this summons myself. Well before the next announcement the Executive Officer (XO) was standing in sickbay screaming at us to get dressed and report to the quarterdeck. He yelled something about us being in deep crap and something about an admiral.

When we got to the quarterdeck, our friend from the night before was having a friendly chat with the CO. As we approached, the CO looked as if he would shoot us both if he had a weapon. Our friend smiled and said you guys ready to go fishing? The CO was behind our friend and was shaking his head in the affirmative. Of course we said yes. And off we went on our fishing trip.

During the fishing trip our newly found friend explained why the CO was so upset. We came to find out that our friend was a retired vice admiral and had been the Chief of Naval Personnel at the time of his retirement. Rodney and I knew that all the explaining in the world was not going to get the XO off of our ass when we returned to the ship. We did not catch many fish and spent the day trying to determine what the worst thing that the CO could do to us. We decided that he could not court martial us, but figured he was going to make our lives hell for a while.

Surprisingly when we returned to the ship our department head, a commander, called us into his office and was laughing when we entered. He said that we were the talk of the ship and that the CO said that if he saw either of us before the ship got back to Charleston he was going to throw us over the side. I guess even a CO can have a sense of humor at times.

****

Upon arriving back to Charleston I was surprised to see June and Dee waiting for me at the head of the pier. We went home and I gave June and Dee the few little things that I had bought for them and our routines were right back in place.

****

Shortly before I got my orders to leave the *Gilmore* I had a freak accident on the way to work one morning. Our home had a carport and I frequently left the windows to our car in the down position. One morning I came out with my hot cup of coffee and left for work. About two miles from the house I was driving down hill on a two lane road when all of a sudden something wet and slimy started to crawl up the inside of my left leg. I did not know what to do. I was holding the hot coffee with one hand and the steering wheel with the other. Well whatever this thing was it was continuing to move towards my crotch. I had slowed the car down some but still had to take action soon or this thing was going to be inside my underpants. The next move in that direction caused me to turn loose of my coffee and it burned my right leg. But the burn was not my concern. With my right hand I started to beat the hell out of this thing that was attacking me. Though I had not been bitten or anything I expected the worse to occur soon. The next think I knew I came to an abrupt halt as I had run into a bridge abutment while not concentrating on my driving.

I was not hurt and immediately jumped out of the car and pulled my pants down to attack this creature that was attacking me. Well it turned out to be one of those little green slimy tree frogs. I had left the windows open and he had availed himself of my front seat. I beat the little damn thing to death right there. During all of this I had not noticed that there was another car pulled up in front of me on the bridge. The red light flashing brought me back to reality. I realized that I had had a wreck and that a policeman was on the scene. When I told him what had happened he laughed so hard that he had to sit down in the front seat of my car. He said he had never seen anything like it. When he had crested the hill he saw that I had run into the bridge and that I was standing in the middle of the road with my pants down, beating myself as if I was trying to knock my leg off. Well he may have thought it was funny but I sure as hell did not. The car was not banged up too badly because at the point of impact I was going less than five miles per hour.

THIRTEEN

S HORTLY AFTER RETURNING FROM SPRING BOARD I RECEIVED orders to
Medical Administrative Technician (MAT) School. The school was
in San Diego. So there we were, going back across Country for a nine
month course.

My weight gain was nil to this point. I was having trouble eating and
found myself drinking more.

June, Dee and I packed up our household goods that were to be shipped
to San Diego then packed what we needed for the trip across Country. We
made the trip a vacation of sorts in that we tried to see anything of interest
on the way.

We were assigned government quarters on the Naval Training Center at
Point Loma. The quarters were nothing to brag about, and we settled in—
beat-up government issued furniture and all.

Once classes started I realized that this was going to be a challenging
course of instruction. Our first class was a college level psychology course.
The instructor was a physician. He walked into the class and wrote his
name on the blackboard and then started to write information on it. When
he started on the second blackboard we figured we probably should be
taking notes. When he finished filling up the second blackboard he went
back to the first and erased everything he had written. And then he started
to write again. This continued for the entire one hour and fifteen minutes
of the class. When class was over he still had not uttered a word, and he
walked out of the classroom.

We discussed this strange behavior and decided to put a stop to it. The
next day when he entered the classroom he looked up and down the chalk
tray under the two blackboards and there was no chalk. We knew we had
him now. Surprise, surprise, he was not new to this tactic and reached into

his jacket pocket and came out with a stick of chalk and started to write. This crazy behavior continued for the next four classes. We were finger sore from taking notes.

At the beginning of the fifth class he came in and said, "Put away all notes and books and take pencil and paper out. We are having a quiz." I think the high score on the quiz was something like a sixteen. He had our attention. We knew that we were not going to be spoon fed information and that we had better study what was provided and be prepared for a quiz every day.

We settled in and started to work together to get through this demanding course of studies.

We were taught everything we would need to know to manage a major naval hospital. Everything from supply, to personnel records, to engineering, to public speaking, to patient records to judicial matters. Thrown in were college level courses in writing, psychology, and accounting. The homework requirement was unbelievable.

****

I noticed that something was changing with June. She never got up before I left for class each day and I was still changing and feeding Dee before I left. I then put Dee back into bed with June. When I started to come home and find June still in her night clothes and Dee apparently not being taken care of I started to worry. As I neared the end of my course of instruction, June became delusional. I could not even have a rational conversation with her. I went to one of the physician instructors on the staff and asked for advice.

He recommended that I take June to the base clinic and have her evaluated by a physician. When I suggested that June go with me to the clinic she went berserk.

I got through my final exams and finished fourth out of a class of fifteen. The school staff knew that I was having problems and excused me from the last two days of the administrative drill associated with getting ready to transfer.

On the advice of one of the clinic doctors I was to try and get June to go with me to see one of the base chaplains. He said that he would give the chaplain a heads up that June was a potential psychotic and that if the chaplain agreed he would give the clinic physician a call and he would contact the civilian authorities to determine how to deal with the issue.

I was surprised when June agreed to go with me to meet with the chaplain. We were about thirty minutes into our meeting when the chaplain asked if we would excuse him for a minute. He went out and called the clinic physician and told him that June was in dire need of mental health assistance. He came back into the room and continued to try and humor June for almost an hour. Suddenly there was a knock on the chaplain's door and when he opened it the clinic physician was standing there with several civilian policemen. June immediately physically attacked the chaplain. The civilian policemen came in and restrained her. They called for a civilian ambulance and requested that a doctor meet the ambulance at the local hospital to determine if she required a competency decision. I broke down in tears as they took her away screaming and fighting them all the way. Unfortunately, Dee was being watched by one of the chaplain's assistants and saw her mom being physically carried out to an ambulance. I gave the police my phone number and asked where they were taking her. He gave me the name of the hospital and they left. Dee and I went back to our government quarters. I called the school and explained what was going on and they said that I did not have to come to the school until I had things under control.

I did not know where to turn. I finally called June's mother, Donna, and explained what had happened and asked her if she would come to San Diego and help me deal with June and Dee. She arrived the next day.

I tried to explain what had happened, and June's mom said that she had experienced similar strange behavior before, but nothing like this. With her mom helping with Dee, and the understanding of the school staff, I was going to now be able to spend time at the hospital. However, I was not allowed to visit and was told that June was heavily medicated. The decision was made to move her to a local psychiatric hospital. After the transfer I went to the new hospital and met with her doctor. He said that he thought it would be best if we gave her a week for them to try and stabilize her before either her mom or I were to visit.

After a week the doctor decided that having her mom visit would be better than having me visit. After a couple of successful visits with her mom I was invited to come along. I was surprised that June showed little animosity towards me. She asked why I had done this to her and the doctor shook his head in the affirmative and I said that I thought she needed help that I was not able to give her. She seemed to accept this answer and to my surprise seemed fairly normal. Later the doctor said that he felt that with continued medication and visits from her mom and me, June could possibly be released within a week to ten days.

Almost two weeks later the doctor released June and gave her mom some medication that he said June needed to continue. And he wrote up a consult for June to continue care when we got to our next duty station.

****

I don't know how I got through all of this with my stomach getting worse and the blood in my bowel movements increasing. I was afraid to mention any of this because I didn't want to be hospitalized and separated from June and Dee. Especially with June's condition still somewhat unstable.

I had received orders to the Base Clinic at Naval Air Station, Oceana, Virginia Beach, Virginia. I was authorized fourteen days leave and with my travel time of three days plus two days proceed time I had almost three weeks before I had to report in.

It was agreed that June would fly home with her mom and Dee, and that I would fly home as soon as I could sell our car.

I hated to sell my car as it was the nicest car that I had ever owned. I got a fair price for it and flew to Columbia, S.C. the next day. June, Dee and her mom met me at the airport and we spent a couple days at her Mom's house.

June decided that she wanted to visit with her dad and since I had not met him I thought that might be a good idea. The man was also crazy.

We borrowed June's mom's car to drive to Greenwood, S.C. where her dad lived. His first comment was why we were driving her mom's car. When we explained what had happened, he asked me if I had a couple of hundred dollars to buy a good used car. June and I had a little money, but I was a little concerned with her dad's mental condition. We bought an old 1954 Ford that ran but was not in the best condition. Her dad said not to worry because we were not keeping that car. I was more than a little confused.

He took me to a local auto tire dealer and had all new tires put on the car. I asked, "Why we would do that if we were not keeping the car?" He winked and said, "Trust me." After the tires were on the car he drove me to a local car lot. We waited around until a salesman noticed us and asked what we were looking for. Well by then we had found a 1962 Mercury that was in pretty good condition, except for the tires.

The bargaining began. Our strongest selling point for trading in my '54 Ford was the four brand new tires. The salesman was impressed with the tires and with the car lot owner's blessings we got a heck of a deal on that car.

As we left with the Mercury with the bad tires I was still confused about what was going on. Well Dad said not to worry he had things under control.

I awoke the next morning with Dad's advice that June and I get on the road ASAP. When I went out to the Mercury I noticed that it had four brand new tires on it. He had actually gone back to the car lot during the night and had stolen the new tires off of the '54 Ford. With June driving her mom's car and me driving the one that was probably going to send me to prison we left Greenwood just as the sun was coming up.

I had never been involved in anything such as this, with the possible exception of stealing an entire car. June thought it was a big lark. She told me that her dad was capable of doing almost anything.

After depositing her mom's car back in Columbia we headed out to Virginia Beach and our new home. It took us a couple of days before we found a place to live and had our household goods delivered.

FOURTEEN

I CHECKED INTO THE BASE CLINIC AND MET ONE OF THE biggest Sailors I had ever met. Ralph was 6'5" and weighed near 300 pounds. He was overweight, but he was also just a big man. We almost immediately became lasting friends. He was senior to me, but I had the benefit of the MAT school training so I essentially was responsible for everything except the patient appointment schedule.

Ralph was married but they had no children. He had grown up in Hazard, Kentucky. His background in a coal mining town was not much different from mine in a cotton mill town.

About four weeks after arrival, June and I were assigned base housing, which was an apartment type structure with two floors. We got settled and I tried to get on with my duties at the clinic.

One morning I was having a lot of problems with my stomach and did not realize it until Ralph noticed that I had black crap on the back of my trousers. I told him that I had been bleeding for some time and that I was just hoping things would get better. I didn't need health problems with June appearing to be improving.

Ralph insisted that I see one of the clinic doctors about my stomach. The doctor examined me and asked me how much did I weigh? I told him around 145 pounds. He asked if this was my normal weight. I told him that I weighed about 185 pounds when I went to Vietnam but had lost a lot of weight and was not regaining it. He made an appointment for me for the following day with the gastroenterologist at Portsmouth Naval Hospital.

When I came home that night June hit me with some more brain-rattling news. She was pregnant. This was April of 1970. I made the mistake of not telling her about my doctor's appointment the following day. We celebrated with a night at the base club for dinner and drinks.

I got dressed and drove over to the hospital the next morning for my appointment. The gastroenterologist ordered a number of blood test and made me an appointment for two days hence when the test results would be back.

I went home and decided not to share this information with June. The next day I went to work and put in a full day. I had told Ralph about the follow-up appointment the following day.

When I reported to the hospital to see the doctor the next day he told me that he was admitting me. "Admitting me, what the hell for?" He said that I had a serious gastrointestinal problem. His initial diagnosis was that my intestines had been invaded with some form of Strongyloides parasite. I asked what that meant and he described my symptoms perfectly. He said that burning pain, tissue damage, sepsis, and ulcers could occur. In severe cases, edema may result in obstruction of the intestinal tract, as well as loss of peristaltic contractions. Then he really floored me when he told me that the parasite was not my only intestinal issue, I also was supporting a tape worm.

This sounded pretty serious to me and when he said he was transferring me to Naval Hospital Bethesda, Maryland, for treatment I knew things were going to get worse before they got better. I expected to go home and get some clothes and at least get a chance to explain things to June. He said that I was not leaving the hospital; that they were transporting me by ambulance to Bethesda. Now he had my attention. Why an ambulance? He said that I could not be transported with IVs in my arm any other way.

I called the clinic and told Ralph what was going on and that June did not know anything about all of this. I also told him that June was pregnant. Ralph told me to not to worry about anything and that he would tell June of the situation and help her in any way he could.

I arrived at Bethesda that evening and was admitted. I called June and she said that Ralph had come by and that she and Dee were doing well. She never asked me how I was doing or how long this situation might last.

When we hung up I was more concerned than ever. She did not sound right. I was worried that she was not taking her medication and was backsliding in her mental health.

Long story short, I was hospitalized at Bethesda and Portsmouth hospitals for ten months. After admission they indicated that they needed to deal with the tape worm prior to dealing with the parasite.

With the decision to get rid of the tape worm first, they indicated that I was going to be sick as hell for a week or so. I found out that to get rid of the tape worm they had to kill it first. To do that they gave me what was basically "rat" poison in small, but increasing doses. Eventually, after feeling like crap for days, I and my squiggly friend parted ways. The passing of the tape worm is something I will always remember. With the assistance of one of the doctors he came out—dead. So now they decided to work on the parasite problem.

I spoke with June from time to time but she never visited. Bethesda treated me with some type of medication that was worse than the illness, I was constantly dizzy and vomiting, and got to where I could give a crap if I lived or died. The doctor explained that this would be a repeated treatment because it only killed the adult parasites and therefore as new ones hatched we needed to continue killing them. I thought they were killing me.

Shortly after one of these treatments I awoke to find a new patient in the bed to my left. He was moaning and was strapped to the bed with leather restraints. A couple of days later they removed the restraints and he propped himself up on one elbow and asked, "What is wrong with you"? I told him that the hospital staff was trying to kill me. He laughed.

I said, "What's so funny?"

He said, "I'm in here for just the opposite; I'm trying to kill myself."

I found out that he was a medically retired Marine sergeant who had been severely wounded in Vietnam, after I had already left following my second tour.

He had lost a kidney, the sight in one eye and part of his left foot. He had undergone something like twenty surgeries. He was addicted to the pain medications when he was discharged and immediately found an illegal supply in the Washington, D. C. area. He told me that this was his third, or maybe fourth admission for drug related problems since he had been discharged from the Marines. When the police discovered he was a retired Marine they brought him to Naval Hospital Bethesda. As time went on he improved to the point where they discharged him. As he left, he said,

"If they don't kill you and you stay here long enough I'll see you again soon." I don't recall seeing him again, but it made me wonder what happened to him and how many more were out there dealing with the same war related issues.

My Marine friend was replaced by another Marine who had been severely wounded in Vietnam. He had lost his lower jaw and was wearing a rubber mask across his lower jaw area. What made him truly interesting was that he was a smoker and learned to smoke by sticking his cigarettes up his nose to inhale. He was only there for a few days as he was moved to an orthopedic ward for reconstructive surgery on his face.

Eventually the decision was made to open me up and see what they might find. What the hell, at this point I could have cared less what they did. My wife obviously either was crazy as hell or, best case, did not love me.

Once inside they noticed some damage to my small intestines and removed a portion. Since they had me under anesthesia and on a ventilator they gave me a significant dose of penicillin. I guess I reacted rather violently to the penicillin but they were able to keep me under control until my seizure subsided.

When I woke up I felt like someone had beaten the living crap out of me. I could not move that something didn't hurt. Because of the removal of part of my small intestines I was not given anything to eat for three days, then only liquids for a couple of days and then a soft diet.

When I started to eat I reacted with hives all over my body. The doctors decided that since I was allergic to penicillin they had probably activated something in my body that caused me to become allergic to other things.

An allergist did scratch tests on me and determined that I was in fact allergic to numerous things. A cocktail of different allergy medications was prepared and I started to receive injections under my skin twice a day. This continued for two months and then was reduced to once a day.

As I improved physically the decision was made to return me to duty in a "light duty" status and to let Naval Hospital Portsmouth, Virginia, manage my progress.

Two days later I was home and June no longer had that "girlie" figure that I was accustomed to. It was also obvious that she had regressed in her mental state to the point where I could not communicate with her. She had the eyes of a rabid dog most of the time and either ignored me or screamed and hollered constantly. I could not get her to take her medicine and she sure as heck was not going to the clinic to see a doctor.

As fate would have it, she showed up at the clinic one afternoon in her pajamas and commenced to create an unbelievable scene. One of the doctors called security on the base and they sent a paddy wagon and three Masters-at-Arms. With the doctor's consent they physically strapped her to one of the clinic gurneys. The doctor called the local hospital and requested permission to transport her to that facility. The hospital had to get all the legal issues resolved before they could accept her. All of this took about two hours. During that period June broke free of her restraints—twice.

June was admitted to the Virginia Beach General Hospital Psychiatric Unit. They would not let me visit her, but on the fifth day of her hospitalization, 14 November 1970, I received a call from the hospital to inform me that June had just delivered a baby girl. I asked if I could come to see her and was told that she was in the maternity ward and could receive visitors.

When I got there they took me to June's room and she seemed happy to see me. She was holding the most beautiful, ugly thing I had ever seen. We talked and she said that her "other" doctor had indicated that when the maternity ward was willing to release her she could come home. She said she had scheduled four follow-up appointments with the psychiatrist. I was relieved and confused about how she had recovered so quickly, but I wanted her at home. I had been taking Dee to a sitter every day and taking care of her when I was not working. Some "light duty" this was!

****

Three weeks after June was back in the house I pulled a weekend duty. I reported Saturday morning and was relieved Monday morning. After being relieved I had to work the normal work day. I had tried all weekend to get in touch with June via the phone but she never answered. At lunch time on Monday I ran home to make sure everything was okay. Surprise, surprise! June was not there and neither was anything else. She had left the military furniture and that was it. I was stunned.

I called Ralph and asked if he could come over to my house for a few minutes. He arrived shortly. He did not seem surprised. His first words to me were, "Good riddance. Hugh," he said, "you are so fortunate to be rid of that crazy woman."

I rounded up all my personal belongings and with Ralph's assistance turned in the family housing key and moved into the barracks.

****

One really interesting event occurred during this tour. Ralph and I became avid fly fishermen for largemouth bass. The fish camp we launched his boat from was run by a retired first class petty officer. He was not the sharpest knife in the drawer and we enjoyed playing jokes on him. He was good natured but we found that he was extremely lonely. He said during one conversation that he had never had a girlfriend in his life. Well Ralph looked at me and said, "Hugh, we can fix this."

When we got home Ralph dug out an old magazine that had a section where women in Haiti were looking to immigrate to the U.S. and were willing to marry an American to do so. Ralph called a local lawyer and explained the magazine article to him. He assured Ralph that if an American were to go to Haiti and legally marry a Haitian national they could legally bring them into the States. Well Ralph worked the issue until he found what he considered might be the right match for our lonely guy.

Sam made contact with the agency in Haiti and made arrangements for our guy to meet with our choice. Then we talked to our lonely friend and we were not surprised when he not only agreed to the arrangement but had the funds to make the trip. Ralph gave him all the contact information and we let nature take its course.

Two months later we arrived to launch our boat and our friend introduced us to his new wife. She was considerably darker than our friend and had a six-year-old son, but it was obvious that they were deeply in love.

Ralph suggested that we get into the matchmaking business; I suggested that we quit while ahead.

****

A new chapter was beginning in my life and now there were new choices to make.

FIFTEEN

J UNE HAD TAKEN THE OLD MERCURY WITH HER SO I had to go buy a car.
I bought a little Chevrolet Vega.

When the divorce papers showed up I signed them and sent them back
to her lawyer. Meanwhile, I contacted a lawyer who grew up in my little
Mill Village. I, like every other idiot from the village, was always able
to get Henry to represent me, though he knew he would never collect a
penny for his help.

When I showed up in court for the divorce hearing it was quick and
simple. I did not contest anything and was ordered to pay $179.00 per
month in child support.

As I tried to leave the judge told me to wait. I looked around and there
were two County Sheriff's deputies coming towards me. Henry asked
the judge what was going on. The judge said that I had not paid my taxes
on the Mercury for the past year and that a warrant was out for my arrest.
The fact that June had the car didn't matter; it was registered in my name.
The taxes were $45.00. I did not have $45.00 so I thought, Oh hell, I'm
on my way to jail. Henry requested that the judge be reasonable and give
me the opportunity to pay the taxes within a week. The judge agreed to
that stipulation. June was really enjoying this. She got the car as part of
the divorce settlement, I was stuck with the past taxes and if the judge
had not granted Henry's request I would be in jail. When we got outside,
Henry took me aside and asked if there was any reason that I needed to
visit the State of South Carolina again in the next five years? I had no
immediate family in the state except Dee and Jean, and I wasn't sure that
I wanted to visit them if it meant dealing with June. I told him no, though
I knew that I would be coming back to see the kids. He said, "Okay, get

in your car and get out of the state. If you have to transit the state in the next five years drive carefully because there will be a bench warrant out for you."

As luck would have it, even though I did visit with the kids, I never heard another thing about the taxes.

Hugh's highschool football team, the Olympia Red Devils. Hugh is in the second row from the top, far right, #46, 1960.

Boot camp, Great Lakes, Illinois, 1961.

Honorable Discharge

from the Armed Forces of the United States of America

This is to certify that

RECRUIT (E-1) HUGH CORNELIOUS SULLIVAN JR   25 119 385

Headquarters & Headquarters Company 151st Signal Battalion

was Honorably Discharged from the ARMY NATIONAL GUARD OF

South Carolina

AND AS A RESERVE OF THE ARMY

on the 4th *day of* June 1961

This certificate is awarded as a testimonial of Honest and Faithful Service

THIS DISCHARGE DOES NOT RELIEVE THE INDIVIDUAL NAMED HEREIN FROM ANY RESERVE OBLIGATION TO WHICH HE
MAY BE SUBJECT UNDER THE PROVISIONS OF THE UNIVERSAL MILITARY TRAINING AND SERVICE ACT, AS AMENDED

Major General
The Adjutant General
REPLACES NGB FORM 55 DATED 1 JAN 53, WHICH IS OBSOLETE

NGB FORM 55
1 JULY 59   * GPO : 1959—O—515673   GPO 802531

Hugh's honorable discharge certificate from the South Carolina National Guard, 1961.

Photo taken during humanitarian duty
at Naval Hospital Beaufort, 1965.

Returning from chow at the beginning of
the Monsoons, Vietnam, 1967.

"Main Street," Chu Lai, Vietnam.

DOC!

Hugh with the young Vietnamese orphan nicknamed "Short Round," Vietnam, 1966.

Hugh (*center, with cap*) on MedCap in local village, Vietnam, 1966.

Hugh (*right*) cooking lobster, 1st MarDiv HQ, Vietnam, 1967.

Photo of Hugh taken by a Vietnamese photographer in DaNang, 1967.

Hugh (*top row, 5th from left*) and the ServLant softball team, 1973.

Hugh with wife Wanda on the occasion of Hugh's promotion to ensign, August 1976.

Hugh and Wanda attending an event honoring Medal of Honor recepient the late Robert Bush (*center*), 1988.

Commander Hugh Sullivan during Operation Desert Storm, Kuwait, March 1992.

Hugh in captured Iraqi-Russian-made tank. Note the black of the burning oil wells in the background. Operation Desert Storm, Kuwait, 1992.

SIXTEEN

P HYSICALLY I WAS ON THE MEND. I WAS GAINING some weight back and while I missed my kids I felt free of June at last.

I had too much free time so I started to tend bar at one of the military clubs. At some point I think I was drinking as much as I was serving. I was running on about four hours sleep a night, but my work day at the clinic never suffered. In fact I was selected as the "Sailor of the Month" for the entire base, twice in a six month period.

A shapely waitress at the club, by the name of Brenda, started to take interest in me and I was easily captured. She had one of those smiles that made you think that she knew something about you that you didn't know yourself. We went together rather steadily for about six months. She was divorced and had custody of her two young boys.

****

A new Navy program was announced where the Navy was seeking applicants from E-6 personnel to go to a junior college and obtain an associate degree. I applied, and to my surprise I was selected. I was also surprised when I found out that I was going to Pensacola, Florida, to attend the Pensacola Junior College.

I detached in October of 1970 and was scheduled to start classes in the January semester.

When I informed Brenda about this she was stunned, but very quickly congratulated me and said, "That's okay, we can work this out." She said nothing else up to the day I departed for Pensacola, when she said, "I'll see you soon." I was not sure what she meant but did not give it much thought.

I took a couple of weeks leave and looked around the Pensacola area. I had been there once before when I was still in high school to visit with my sister Florence but did not remember much about it. Pensacola could be described as several different towns. The downtown area was historic and beautiful. The area near the main base, Naval Air Station (NAS), Pensacola, was typical in that there was a bar next door to a tattoo parlor, next door to a bar. This ran for at least six blocks from the front gate of NAS. And then there was the beach area which was the most beautiful beach in the world. The sand was the color of sugar. When you walked on it the sand made a squeaking noise.

I found that I was not required to live on base and I found a small duplex close to the junior college and not too far from NAS or the beaches. It was furnished, but I still needed to go out and buy some basic stuff. I had a phone installed. I thought, this is going to be great.

The day before I was to check in to Corry Naval Base, where my personnel records would be kept, I received a phone call. It was Brenda announcing that she and her two boys had just arrived in town. Holy crap, now I understood what she meant when she said "We can work this out" and "I will see you soon."

I went to the motel and while I had reservations about this meeting I was happy to see her and the boys. I had never tried to be a father to the two boys, but I had always been nice to them.

Brenda and I talked for a while and then I told her that I had to go because I had some last minute issues to resolve before I reported to Corry for my meeting with the OIC of the students. He was responsible for ensuring that we took the proper courses and he reviewed our semester grades. We would have to maintain at least a 3.0 average and enroll in at least fifteen semester hours, or we would be pulled from school and sent back to the fleet.

Brenda said she understood and that she had planned to look for a place for her and the two boys to live as soon as possible. As I left there was the perfunctory hug and kiss, but I realized that I felt nothing emotionally that could turn into something permanent.

The following day I reported to the personnel office at Corry and was directed to a lady sitting in the back, right-hand corner of the large personnel office. She was responsible for taking care of all Associate Degree Completion Program (ADCOP) records.

As I approached her desk I realized that I was looking at one of the most beautiful women I had ever seen. She looked up and said, "Are you a new ADCOP Student?" I must have looked like a complete dolt because I just stood there admiring her beauty and did not hear a word she said. Finally out of the fog I realized she was asking for my records and orders. She asked me to have a seat in the chair next to her desk.

I sat and waited for her to review my orders and check to ensure that all of my records were in order. She informed me that there were two more ADCOP students due in today and that the lieutenant (LT) who was going to be our reporting senior had a get-together scheduled for all of us tomorrow. She said she would get me all checked in and ensure that if I needed money I would have the opportunity to see the disbursing clerk that managed my record.

While all of this was going on I looked her over very carefully. I noticed that she was not wearing a wedding ring. My first thought was that she might be preparing to become a nun, or, God forbid, she was gay.

As she reviewed my records I realized that she was going to know a heck of a lot more about me than I was going to know about her. So I took the initiative. I told her that I also had two dependent daughters. She said, "So I noticed." I asked her if she was married. She looked at me for probably the first time with any kind of interest. She said, "Why do you ask"? Without even thinking I said, "Because before I leave here you and I are going to have at least one date." She smiled and said, "We will see."

I had not been completely cut off. I asked how often I would be required to meet with the LT. She said other than tomorrow I would only need to see him if I was having some kind of problem. "He will leave you alone as long as you do your school work and do not have problems with the local authorities," she told me.

Getting braver, I asked, "How often do I need to see you?"

She laughed and said, "Not too often."

She looked at me as if she expected a reply so I gave her one. "You can expect to see me frequently. I will find a need to discuss something in my record more often than you might think."

"Concentrate on your studies and don't waste time chasing skirts."

I could not resist it: "You are no skirt, you are something special."

"They all say something like that," she said, "but at least you're single."

With that she said that she had endorsed my orders having me report in at 1300 today. I said, "And"? She said that she had nothing else for me so I could leave. "Just be here at 0800 tomorrow morning to meet with the lieutenant," were her parting words.

As I left I knew that poor Brenda had hitched her wagon to the wrong horse. I also knew that I had to share this with her as soon as possible.

I went back to the motel that Brenda was staying in and she was packing her car and had hitched up the U-Haul trailer with her personal belongings. She informed me that she had signed a three month lease on a two bedroom apartment and was on the way over to move in.

She asked if I would give her a hand moving in. I knew that the longer I let this fester the worse it would get. And, after meeting Wanda I knew that Brenda would never be able to compete.

I told her that I was sorry to hear that she had made a financial commitment to stay in Pensacola because I was not going to be able to spend much time with her. I could see in her eyes that she understood what I was saying. She said, "Well, I can't afford to pay the lease and have enough money to return to Norfolk." Besides, she had leased her house in Norfolk and had nowhere to live even if she got back to Norfolk.

I tried to think. I was not wealthy but I did have a little cash put aside from my bar tending days and my monthly salary. I asked, "How much is the lease her for?" She told me it was $140.00 per month and that she had already paid the first month's rent. That left $280.00 due for the remaining two months. I told her that I could not pay all of the remaining monies due but I could give her $200.00. She looked at me with tears in her eyes and said, "I don't need your help."

I left her there in the parking lot of the motel not only feeling like a jerk, but knowing that I *was* a jerk. Though I had not encouraged or asked her to come to Pensacola I felt responsible. I asked her where the apartment was located. She gave me the name of the apartments and I knew where they were.

I left the motel before she did and went to the apartments and found the manager. I explained that Brenda had just signed a three month lease and had paid the first months lease. I asked him if he would release her from the last two months if I gave him $200.00. He wanted to know what was going on and I half-assed explained that she had followed me to Pensacola from the Norfolk, Virginia, area with the thought in mind that she and I would eventually get married or at least live together. I assured him that I had no intentions of having her follow me to Pensacola, but that I felt responsible for her situation. He turned out to be a very nice man. He said that if it was agreeable with Brenda he would void her lease and charge her a daily rate until she could get things together to return to Norfolk.

Brenda arrived and saw me talking to the manager. She came over and said that I did not speak in her behalf. The manager told her what he was willing to do and she looked stunned. She told him that if it was okay with him she would be returning to Norfolk the next day. He refunded her lease money and tore up the lease. I figured this was a good time for me to exit.

While sometime in the future I would see Brenda again we never spoke another word to each other.

SEVENTEEN

IT WAS NOVEMBER OF 1970 AND I REPORTED to the lieutenant the following morning and found out that there were thirty of us starting classes in January for the winter semester. I also found out that we had the entire period off from the end of the fall semester, early December, until the beginning of the winter semester, mid-January, without charged leave. That amounted to almost two months of free time!

Christmas came and went and I was getting bored. Finally I got the courage to ask Wanda to go out with me on New Year's Eve. Surprisingly, she accepted--conditionally. The condition was that we double dated with her best friend. I would have double dated with Adolph Hitler to get Wanda out on a date. She told me where she would like to spend New Year's Eve, and I went right then and purchased four tickets. I went back and gave her two for her friend and her date. As it turned out her friend's date decided they were a gift because I never got my money back.

I was still considerably underweight and needed to purchase something fitting for the occasion. I went to Sears and purchased a nice off-the-rack suit, a white shirt, shoes and socks, a necktie and a belt. I was ready to go.

That date is etched in my mind forever. I picked Wanda up at her mom's house. Her mom was babysitting Wanda's daughter, Jamie, and it gave Wanda a chance to let her mom check me out. I guess I passed because she didn't suggest that Wanda stay home.

We danced and had a great time. When it was time to go home I got the expected kiss goodnight. I went home in a daze.

****

We were required to carry a class load of fifteen semester hours and we had limited major fields of study that we could concentrate on. Of course there were a number of humanity courses required by the college and around the core course requirements the LT would approve our electives. I figured that I would pursue business courses and the LT approved my schedule once I had it nailed down with the school.

Being the smart guy that I am I looked at when the courses that I wanted to take were available and as it worked out I was able to schedule all my classes on Tuesdays, Wednesdays, and Thursdays. That left me with Friday through Monday free to do homework, find excuses to go see Wanda and fish.

****

The first day of school is an orientation day where they explain a lot of things that do not necessarily pertain to the academic portion of the school. As I sat there I became a little concerned. While in Vietnam I had taken a number of U.S. Armed Forces Institute (USFI) college level courses. I had done fairly well on them, but I was afraid they might not be the same as attending college. I thought back to one of my fourth grade report cards where the teacher had given me an overall grade of D-, but in the comments section she had written a note to my parents that stated, "Hugh has shown remarkable improvement during this marking period." I thought how the heck could someone show remarkable improvement with a D- grade?

I found out quickly that I and the other ADCOP students were six to ten years older than the other students on campus and that we had solid work habits because of our military backgrounds. While the classwork was challenging at times we solidly outperformed the younger students. Maintaining a 3.0 average was not going to be a problem. And working three days a week was a blessing. I fished and periodically pestered Wanda for a date and still had plenty of time to keep up my classwork. By the end of the winter semester I was a solid 3.5 student.

The school year went by fairly quickly and here we were at the holidays again. Again, I asked Wanda out for New Year's Eve, and again she accepted and suggested we double date with her friend again. Her friend had a different date than the previous year and I really enjoyed his company. At the time we did not know it but Wanda's friend and her date were to be married about six months after Wanda and I were married, and Wanda's friend (Fred) and I were to become lasting friends and fishing buddies. It was a most enjoyable and memorable night that ended again with a goodnight kiss.

The second and final year of my junior college career was not much different than the first except during the summer semester my oldest sister, Florence, and her husband, John, were coming to Pensacola to pick up their middle son, Ben, who had spent several weeks with me. Florence said that she and John would like to go out dancing one night while they were in Pensacola. They had lived in Pensacola when John was a young sailor. I thought back on the time that my mom and I had visited them when I was still in high school.

The only girl that I had met since arriving in Pensacola that I would even consider taking on a double date with my sister was Wanda. You don't know unless you ask!

I called Wanda that night and after a little small talk I explained about my sister and her husband's visit and desire to go out dancing. I asked her if she would be willing to go with me. She asked why I was asking her. I told her that she was the only decent girl that I knew in Pensacola. She laughed and said, "How can I turn down that offer"?

The date was one of those magical moments. After two New Year's Eve dates where nothing happened, the sparks flew on this date. We sat in the backseat of John's car and when we kissed it was like trumpets blaring, whistles blowing and lightning flashing.

That was late June. Wanda and I were married on August 4, 1972. We had a simple wedding in the chapel at Corry Station and were married by the base chaplin.

****

In early December of 1972 Wanda and I went to visit my two daughters. This would be the first meeting for them. We took Christmas presents because we did not think we would be back before the holidays. So we had an early Christmas for them. I was somewhat surprised when we explained to Wanda's daughter, Jamie, that she would not have any presents because hers were in Pensacola. She did not have any problems with this. The visit was nice. Dee and Jean enjoyed their presents and seemed to really get along well with Jamie. After the visit we headed home to Pensacola with a feeling that maybe we could make all of this work.

A week after our return to Pensacola I was surprised when June's mom called me and asked if I was willing to take charge of Dee and Jean? I asked her what was the problem and she said that June was in the local mental hospital and that she could not take care of the kids. I told her that I would get back to her within the hour.

I found Wanda and explained the situation and without hesitation she said you are out of school for the holidays so we will go get them tomorrow. I was shocked.

When we got to Donna's home in North Augusta, South Carolina, she had the kids packed and we didn't even stay in town, but drove a hundred miles or so toward Pensacola before we found a motel for the night.

Wanda and I knew that this decision was going to cost us. They still believed in Santa Claus so we now had to buy a second round of Christmas gifts for Dee and Jean so that they could enjoy Christmas with Jamie.

Two weeks later I received a court summons from the Pensacola Family Court. I had been charged with kidnaping.

Three days later when we went to court, Donna was sitting in the front row in front of the judge reading the Bible. The judge dropped the kidnaping charges and returned custody to June; Donna swore that she had never asked us to come get the girls. I was told that I would have to pay the expenses for June and her mother's visit to Pensacola. This came to almost $300.00. That pretty much wiped out our saving account.

Wanda not once said she had any regrets and if the situation came up again we would respond the same way. I thought, "I don't think so."

****

We also had problems with Wanda's ex-husband. He gave Wanda some lip the first time he came to get Jamie after our marriage. I stepped in front of Wanda and told him that from that moment on he would be dealing with me, not Wanda. He huffed up but that is what the future held and we never had any more problems with him.

****

That spring, after graduation and before I was to start my leave, Wanda called and said that my detailer wanted to talk to me about orders. I went to the base and sitting at her desk called my detailer. Wanda and all her friends were crowded around her desk waiting to see where we would be going.

Wherever we were going, we were going as a chief petty officer as I had been selected for promotion.

Wanda had never been out of the state of Florida, except to lower Alabama, which was less than twenty miles away, and I knew she had no concept about what she had signed on for. I tried as best I could to explain to her what to expect with regards to moving and getting settled in a new place, but I knew I was not getting through.

When the detailer told me where we were going I guess I went white, in spite of the deep tan that I had acquired fishing almost every day. As I hung up the phone I just sat there. Wanda said, "Well where are we going?"

"I don't know."

"What do you mean you don't know"?

I said, "I've never heard of the place."

"Where, where?"

"Asmara, Ethiopia."

"Where is that?"

We all ran to the wall map of the world and someone was smart enough to know that it was somewhere in Africa. We found it, eventually. Wanda was in shock. I told her to not panic until we had more information about the place.

That day after work Wanda went to the local library and checked out the only two books that mentioned Ethiopia.

When I came home she was sitting at the kitchen table with tears coming like buckets. When I asked what was wrong she said, "Everything I read about Ethiopia is bad. They suggest you leave the windows open when running water because the water had toxic fumes that could be harmful if inhaled. The only school was on the base and covered grades 1-12 with teachers teaching multiple grades and subjects. I cannot take my child to a place like this."

I tried to reason with her by pointing out that there were Americans living there right now and I had heard nothing on the news about any of them having any problems. Not much help in overcoming her concerns.

When we decided to get married I told her that when I graduated from school we would more than likely be leaving Pensacola. She either didn't really think about that possibility or she figured we would go to somewhere exotic like Hawaii. I was at a loss.

For almost two weeks we barely communicated without her crying.

Two days before we were to have our household goods packed out Wanda called me at home and said that my detailer and called and wanted me to call him at my earliest convenience. She said, "Your earliest convenience is right now! Get out here."

When I called he told me that Ethiopia had severed diplomatic relations with the United States and that we were closing the base, so I would not be going to Ethiopia.

My look of relief was misinterpreted by Wanda and her gang of friends standing by to see what new torture was to be bestowed on poor Wanda and her young daughter.

When I hung up the phone Wanda just stared at me. Finally I said, "We're not going to Ethiopia." The look of relief on Wanda's face was an unbelievable look of joy. In a concerned voice she said, "Now where are we going?" I told her we were going to the staff of Commander U.S. Service Forces, Atlantic Fleet (ServLant).

After not saying anything for a minute I asked her, "Do you know where that is"? She smiled and said, "No, but I know it is not in Ethiopia."

She asked. "Where is it"? I told her that it was in Norfolk, Virginia.

Well you would have thought that I had told her it was ten miles from Pensacola. She was so happy that she almost broke my back with a hug.

I may be wrong, but I almost believe that had my original orders been to Norfolk she would have been just as upset as she had been over Ethiopia. But after sitting on Ethiopia for two weeks she was elated to be staying in the U.S.

We sold her home two weeks prior to my graduation and transfer, so the day after graduation Wanda, my new best friend Jamie and I headed for Norfolk.

I say my new best friend, because Wanda kept Jamie away from her dates so until our situation became serious enough to discuss marriage I really had not had much of a chance to get to know Jamie. Once we were given the opportunity to get to know each other it was a mutual love affair.

****

When we got to Norfolk we found out that there was a significant waiting list for military quarters. We decided to find something semi-permanent and then start looking for a rental home.

We moved into a one bedroom efficiency apartment that had a small kitchen, an even smaller living room and a tiny bedroom. I watched as Wanda turned this small apartment into a home. I never will forget the first meal she prepared for us there--beef stew. The best meal I could remember and to this day I can still taste it.

Not only did I have a beautiful wife, but one that was a loving mother, a hard working woman, and a great cook. Life was good!

EIGHTEEN

I CHECKED INTO SERVLANT A COUPLE DAYS LATER and found an interesting situation. The ServLant medical and dental officers were actually assigned to the U.S.S. *Vulcan* (AR-5). The *Vulcan* was an auxiliary repair ship that had the ability to repair almost any problems any ship may encounter.

So, I found that the main office in the ServLant building was manned by a master chief hospital corpsman and me.

In the two weeks we were together, the Master Chief showed me how to process medical and dental requests from ships throughout ServLant. It was mostly finding the right office in ServLant to fulfill the requirement and coordinating with that office and the ship requesting assistance.

Two weeks after my reporting the Master Chief transferred. There was no replacement for him, because there was a major reorganization of the Atlantic and Pacific Fleets coming soon.

On his way out the door he gave me the combination to a huge safe in the office. I had really not shown much interest in the safe but one day decided to open it and see what I had inherited. What I inherited was a disaster. The safe was full of narcotics. I mean all prescription drugs including over 200 morphine seriates. This in and of itself would not have been too alarming had there been any kind of paperwork in the safe to help me understand what was in there and where it had come from. I went to work scouring the office files trying to find some kind of inventory list. I found none, but I did find the answer as to where they probably came from.

There had been at least ten ServLant ships decommissioned in the past seven to eight years. And, there was an indication in the files that some equipment was transferred to other ships that could use the equipment.

Putting two and two hundred together I deduced that the drugs were from the ten decommissioned ships. I had no reason to believe that anything other than bad administrative practices had caused this situation, but that did not relieve me of the problem.

I was not sure where to turn, but did not want to get the ServLant Chief of Staff involve yet. I knew that there was a commander MSC serving on the Atlantic Fleet Surgeon's staff, which was one building over from me and I decide to contact him and see what he recommended.

I decided to give the MSC commander a shot and if he was not forthcoming with a solution then I would have to go to my Chief of Staff. The following morning I called the commander and asked if I could have a few minutes of his time to discuss a serious issue. He said to be in his office in ten minutes because he had to be somewhere else in thirty. I got to his office, which was about five minutes away, and started to explain my problem with the safe.

He called his Master Chief in and told him to cancel his appointment with whomever he had an appointment. He then said, "Let's go look at this safe."

When I opened the safe and he saw what was in there he said, "Holy hell!" After a few minutes of looking around and thinking he asked if anyone else was aware of the contents of the safe. I told him that to some extent I had shared this with Wanda and I assumed that the previous Master Chief had some knowledge.

He said, "Okay, here is what we are going to do. You will make a complete inventory of everything in this safe and do not share this information with anyone. When you get the inventory complete give me a call."

It took me a week to finish the inventory. When I called him he said to bring a copy of the inventory over to him.

When I got there I was surprised to see three men in civilian clothing sitting in his office. He introduced me to each of them and referred to each as "doctor." He excused them and asked for the inventory. He was even more surprised when he saw the extent of the drugs in the safe. He explained that the three doctors were coming through Commander in

Chief U.S. Atlantic Fleet (CinCLantFlt) for officer indoctrination and to receive their uniforms. There was no formal program in the Navy for providing physicians and dentist training in what to expect while on active duty. The ones going to ships or foreign shore assignments were provided this indoctrination by the respective fleet surgeons.

He told me to box up all the drugs and break out the inventory list by type with the number of each within each type and to be in his office at 0900 the following day.

I worked until late into the night getting the inventory the way he had requested.

The next morning I called and informed him that I had everything in order. He told me to be in his office at 1300 with the drugs and inventory.

He then asked the Master Chief to muster the three doctors who were there for indoctrination at 1330 in the Fleet Surgeon's head.

The commander had the three doctors lined up in front of the door to the surgeon's head and explained that they were going to witness the destruction of some outdated drugs and participate in flushing them down the toilet.

It took us almost two hours to flush all the drugs and get all three doctors to sign the inventory list certifying that they had witnessed the destruction of all the drugs. The commander retained a copy of the inventory and gave me the signed copy of the original.

I did not know it then, but this was not the last I would see of this commander.

****

Wanda was lucky and found civil service employment at CinCLantFlt.

In Florida, Jamie had started to school at the age of five. In Norfolk kids had to be six to start to school. We got Jamie enrolled in a private school because she had already finished the first grade in Pensacola, but because of her age the Norfolk school system would not let her advance to the second grade.

We soon found a more permanent home and moved in and had our household goods delivered.

Wanda and I spent almost two years at ServLant. Then the reorganization we were awaiting happened. All of the surface type commanders were being consolidated under one commander and the new organization would be called Commander U.S. Surface Force, Atlantic, Fleet. In other words, Commander, U.S. Cruiser/Destroyer Force; Commander, U.S. Amphibious Force; and Commander, U.S. Service Force were going away and would be consolidated into one command.

In spite of the issues with this assignment I was promoted to senior chief petty officer during this tour.

What that meant was that where there had been three force surgeons and their staffs there would now only be one. The Surgeon of U.S. Cruiser/Destroyer Force was designated the Surgeon for the new U.S. Surface Force. He brought with him his staff, and of course that left me without a job.

NINETEEN

I RECEIVED A CALL FROM MY DETAILER AND HE SAID that he was now sending me to the U.S.S. *Simon Lake* (AS-33), home ported in Rota, Spain.

Wanda knew that something was going to happen to us since I did not have a job and surprisingly she took the news of us going to Rota with her chin up and a positive attitude.

The Navy had instituted a new program to help individuals and families adjust to overseas assignments. The program was called "The Navy Sponsor Program." The purpose of the program was to have someone living in the country where the individual and/or family is moving to be available to assist in adapting and adjusting to the new culture and living conditions of the new country.

I did not understand when I received a letter from our sponsor, a master chief hospital corpsman, who was stationed at the base in Rota, rather than someone from the *Simon Lake*. I found out later that the Master Chief asked the ship's medical department if he could be our sponsor as he was ashore and was more able to assist us.

****

Before we left for Rota I was visited by the Navy Investigative Service. They were there to solicit my assistance with a drug ring that was supposed to have its origins aboard the *Simon Lake*. They did not ask that I do anything other than keep my eyes and ears open and gave me a point of contact for their service in Rota. If I even thought that I might have some information I was to pass it along to the Rota contact. I honestly never saw any indication of drug problems during my tour.

****

We flew to Philadelphia and were provided transportation to McGuire Air Force Base for our onward flight to Rota.

When we arrived in Rota our sponsor, a master chief, met us. He was a nice enough guy and helped us load up our bags into his car and drove us to a local hotel about one mile from the front gate at NAS, Rota.

The Rotamar Hotel was nice but much different from its U.S. counterparts. The door knobs were levers versus round like ours. The toilet contained a separate bidet that neither Wanda nor I had seen before. Light fixtures and plugs were 220 volt/50 cycles versus or 110 volt/60 cycles.

Wanda set about getting us settled and we said goodbye to the Master Chief and thanked him for his assistance.

****

On-base housing had a significant waiting list, so we would be looking for some place to live with the locals. Eventually we were moved into on-base housing; with central heat and air conditioning and a phone.

Rota was a fun tour and we enjoyed our stay there. We had a full-time maid and Jamie spent a lot of time with her, so naturally Jamie learned Spanish much faster than Wanda and I. However, I also found out that Wanda had a knack for learning languages and she far exceeded my language skills before we departed Spain.

****

While living off base we had to deal with the local population and the local economy. Wanda was fortunate in that she was able to get a civil service job on the base before I even reported to the Simon Lake. She needed a haircut and went looking for a beauty parlor. When she returned home she was a sight to see and was hysterically crying. I asked her what had happened. She said that she tried to tell the lady that she wanted about one inch removed by showing her with her thumb and first finger. The lady misunderstood and removed all her hair except for about one inch all over. I assured her that it would grow back out and that no one at her new job would know the difference unless she said something.

Wanda's first trip to the butcher was not much better. She wanted to buy some chicken and pork-chops. The chickens still had their heads and feet on them and in her effort to get them removed she confused the butcher to the point where he just quartered the chicken and wrapped it up for her. The pork chops became pork roast. They had never heard of cutting pork in the sizes that she was requesting.

Lastly, we bought a car and it was a stick shift. That was all that was available. I took two days and thought that I had taught Wanda enough to turn her loose with the new car. Wrong! Her first day at work was the day our household goods were to be delivered so she had to drive herself the nineteen miles from home to the base. She had been gone about thirty or forty minutes when she came back into the house crying. After about five minutes she explained that the car had stalled on her and that she could not get it going and had left it and run back home. She said the car was in the middle of the road. I took off running thinking that someone would surely have crashed into it by the time I got there. The farther I ran down the highway the more concerned I became. Finally, about a mile and a half from home, I found the car in the middle of the road as she had said. I got into the car and it started right up. I went back home and Jamie and I gave her a ride to work. I took the chance that the household goods would not be delivered before I returned. Wanda knew that she would just have to wait until I returned that afternoon because we had no phones to communicate.

I thought that with all of this Wanda would want to pack her and Jamie up and head back to the States. Not so, I began to understand that while all was not going the way she wanted or expected, she was truly enjoying the experience of living with a new culture. It was at this point that I realized how fortunate I was to have married Wanda. She was the perfect military wife.

****

Jamie decided that she wanted to play little league baseball. I thought she was talking about the girls' softball league, but no, she was insistent on little league. I worked with her every evening and to my surprise she was not a bad ball player.

When game time came and it was her time to bat all she would do was stand at the plate with the bat on her shoulder. I could not get her to swing the bat no matter what I did. If the pitcher was poor and she got a walk that was the only way she would get on base. Her defensive skills were equal to most of the boys playing. There was only one other girl in the league and she was the star on her team. I was so proud of the way Jamie handled herself throughout the season. The next year she was not interested in playing baseball or softball.

****

Prior to leaving Norfolk I had applied for a commission in the Medical Service Corps. Each year, Navy Medicine selected ten to twenty enlisted for commissioning.

The test was a two-day affair. The first day was a standard test entitled the Officer Selection Battery Test (OSB). This was a general knowledge test that all officer candidates had to pass if they were not graduates of OCS or one of the Service Academies.

If you passed this test then you were eligible for the Medical Service Corps (MSC) Professional Exam. This was a one day test that was totally essay questions. I passed the OSB, so I was able to take the MSC exam.

I got through the first morning of the MSC exam and at lunchtime made a quick run to the base exchange. As luck would have it I had a minor auto accident in the exchange parking lot. After all the paper work was finished, I was an hour late returning for the afternoon session of the exam. They would not allow me to exceed the established time limits so I was not able to finish it. Needless to say, I failed.

However, I had been promoted to Senior Chief and was not too disappointed.

****

After reporting aboard the *Simon Lake* and getting settled, Wanda told me she wanted me to apply for the Medical Service Corps Commission again. I asked why?

I was happy as a senior chief and felt pretty good about the master chief's exam that I had recently taken.

Her reply was she didn't care if I retired as a third class petty officer, she did not want me to quit after failing the MSC exam.

Why argue? So, I applied once more and passed the OSB again and finished the professional exam. The professional exam was tough, but I felt that my education in Medical Administrative School had served me well with regards to answering most of the questions.

Wanda was happy with her civil service employment at the NAS terminal. She had several responsibilities, but keeping the pilot's flight logs was probably her most important function.

****

As time went by, Wanda's sister, Lizzy, got a divorce and asked if she could come visit with us for a couple of weeks. Of course we said yes and were excited about her visit.

In fact we planned a driving trip as far as our money would take us to help Lizzy get her mind off of her situation.

We owned a Volkswagen hatchback and when Lizzy got to Rota we packed it to the gills and set off on our adventure.

The trip was wonderful. We saw a lot of Spain, Andorra, France, and went all the way to Venice, Italy, before heading back to Rota.

We cut it close in that I had half a tank of gas, $1.75 in cash and two apples in our possession when we arrived home to the base. We passed several cars with people we knew and they blew the horn and waved like crazy. We did not know we were loved so much.

A surprise was waiting for us when we got home—a "Naval Message" taped to our front door. The message informed me that I had been selected for commissioning as an ensign in the Medical Service Corps effective 1 August 1976; this was late June. Wanda, Lizzy and Jamie were overjoyed and could not stop hugging me. I was stupefied. There I was, flat broke, no leave and looking at a transfer to God-knew-where in just over a month.

After the initial shock Wanda and I sat down and did the math. Even if I were selected to master chief, which I was, I would not lose money because of a "Loss Pay" provision that says you cannot lose money by being promoted. By the time I was promoted to lieutenant junior grade I would be making more money than I would be staying a master chief. And, every promotion after that was going to mean more money upon retirement.

As hard as it was, we decided to take the commission.

TWENTY

M Y FIRST ASSIGNMENT AS AN OFFICER WAS AS the personnel officer for the National Naval Dental Center in Washington, D.C.

Wanda was able to find work within the civil service system at the Naval Personnel Command in Washington, D.C. She worked for the Prisoner-of-War (POW) Office helping those family members whose spouses were still listed as Missing in Action. It was a very interesting job in that the missing member's pay was still held in hopes of his return. The member had designated what portion of his active duty pay would be given to his spouse if he were to become missing or a POW. Wanda's office was authorized to give the family more than that designated in special circumstances.

My job as the personnel officer was not very challenging. I had ten dental corpsmen working in my personnel office and two, including the leading chief and one first class petty officer, were graduates of the Medical Administrative Technician Course.

Wanda and I bought a nice home with four bedrooms and two and one-half baths.

Just as we were settling in Donna, June's mother, called and gave us the same spiel that we had fallen for in Pensacola. I told her I was hesitant after what she had done to us before. Wanda did not hesitate; she told me that we were going to get the kids.

I called a lawyer in North Augusta, Georgia, and explained the situation and the previous problem with Donna. He said he would take the case and suggested that if she were sincere for her to agree to pay one-half of his fees. He quoted me a fee of $500.00 unless something unforeseen was to come up during the proceedings.

Donna agreed and I took three days leave and Wanda and I headed for North Augusta. The day after we arrived we were in family court. The situation was not only June's mental status, which at the moment was somewhat stable, but the fact that she had a man living with her and the two girls.

The judge listened to all the back and forth and finally decided to postpone his decision for one month. He told June that when we returned in one month that if she still had the man living in her house he was going to give permanent custody of Dee and Jean to me. I thought how unjust this was. I knew that she would move the guy out at least temporarily so as to retain custody.

One month later we were back in court. When the judge asked June if the man was still living with her she said, "Yes and neither you nor anyone else is going to tell me how to live." I could see that the judge was more than a little upset with her attitude. He said, "Okay, effective immediately, full and complete custody of your two daughters is granted to their father." I could not believe it when June asked if she would continue to receive the $179.00 a month that I had been paying for child support. The judge smiled and said, "I'm afraid not."

Oh boy, instant family! The only good news was that we had a house big enough for them. Wanda took to the task like the real classy lady that she is.

****

We settled in and life was almost normal when one day I arrive at work and am told that the CO wanted to see me. I thought, oh crap, what now?

The CO informed me that he had a message stating that all the Command personnel offices were being disestablished and consolidated into one Base Personnel Office. Consequently, my billet had been transferred to this new activity. He indicated that I needed to talk to my detailer.

When I called my detailer I was floored when he indicated that he was transferring me to the Third Marine Division in Okinawa. This was to be a one year, unaccompanied tour. The Vietnam War was over and the Third was back in Okinawa.

I begged him to leave me in the D.C. area because I had a wife and three kids and none of them were comfortable here yet. No go, I was headed to Okinawa.

I told Wanda that night and I also told her that the old commander that had helped me with the drug issue a couple years ago was now the head manpower guy at the Bureau of Medicine and Surgery (BuMed) in D.C., and that I had called and requested an appointment with him the following day. Wanda said, "And what do you think he can do?" I told her I did not know but at least he could clarify for me how this officer crap worked.

When I met with now Captain O'Donnell he listened to my sob story and just smiled. I asked him if he remembered me from Norfolk. He smiled and said of course he did. He advised me to return to work and wait until he could take a look at the situation.

The next morning when I reported to work I was met by the Command's administrative officer and ushered into the CO's Office. The CO was pissed about something and I knew I was the focus of his feelings. He threw a message at me and said, "I don't know how you did this but clean out your desk and get out of my command."

I took the message and left his office. The admin officer was hot on my tail. He said, "Who did you talk to? Your detailer is pissed at you and you had better hope you don't have to deal with him in the future."

I finally had time to read the message and it said that I was to "report immediately" to the Bureau of Medicine and Surgery. I asked the admin officer what that meant. He said he had never seen "report immediately" orders, but they meant that I had to report within twenty-four hours.

I expected a less-than-stellar performance evaluation (Fitness Report) upon my departure but thanks to the admin officer my Fitness Report was outstanding. He convinced the CO that I had nothing to do with the orders. So at least for now my career was not destroyed.

I did not even call Wanda; I packed my desk and drove downtown to BuMed. When I reported into the personnel office I was told to report to Captain O'Donnell.

When I got to his office his secretary said it would be a few minutes before he could see me. About ten minutes later she escorted me into

Captain O'Donnell's office where he was sitting back in his chair, smiling. I was not accustomed to spending much time with captains so I was a little nervous. He asked, "What do you think, Ensign Sullivan?" I was stupefied. I asked him where I was going to be working. He smiled and said, "I have not decided yet, but you are not going to Okinawa." I realized that some of the MSCs had a great deal of influence and had the ability to help or hurt young officers. I would always keep that in the back of my mind when dealing with any senior officer.

As luck would have it three days after reporting, Captain O'Donnell called me to his office and told me that I was going to the Bureau of Naval Personnel (BuPers) to work in a new program that the Navy was starting. The new program was called the Personnel Administrative Support System (PASS). I would be working for a female captain who was in charge. I found out later that the woman was Captain Alexander and when she and Captain O'Donnell were lieutenants they had been good friends. I don't know how "good" their friendship had been, but for me it did not matter.

When I reported to Captain Alexander I found out that the new program was the one that caused me to lose my billet. We were going to close all command personnel offices and merge them into base personnel offices, which would be called Personnel Support Detachments (PSD). All of the PSDs in a geographical area would be subordinated to a Personnel Support Activities (PSA). The senior officer of a PSD would be an Officer-In-Charge (OIC) and the senior officer of the PSA would be a Commanding Officer (CO).

My job was going to be to not only close the Medical Department personnel offices Navy wide, but to help determine which billets in the offices were dedicated to command functions and which were to dedicated to personnel records functions. The command function billets would be returned to the commands and the personnel billets would become part of the new base personnel office. Captain Alexander gave me free range in determining how to do this. However, we did have written authority from the Chief of Naval Operations (CNO) to transfer billets without the command's authority if need be.

This was a very interesting tour of duty. I worked directly with the MSC officers who were serving as the hospital's personnel officers. I explained what they and I had to do and I gave them the opportunity to make the initial decision on the distribution of the existing billets, between command and personnel records functions. I found that almost all were honest and tried to make the decision based upon the functions the person occupying the billet was doing. Some of the people were doing a combination of command and personnel functions. When the personnel officer had the billets distributed according to his evaluation we would go over each billet together. There was some give and take but most of the time we were able to agree with the final analysis.

There were a couple of hospital personnel officers who tried to protect as many of the billets as possible to the point where I had to make some decisions relative to which billets would remain and which would become part of the PASS program. In these contentious situations I analyzed each billet and wrote a justification as to why it should remain with the hospital or go to PASS. On these occasions Captain Alexander supported my analysis completely. There were a couple of upset MSC personnel officers, but had they done what most of their peers had done there would not have been any problems.

For such a junior officer this was really putting me in a situation where I was building a reputation early that would follow me for the remainder of my career. Thank God the personnel officers that worked honestly with me far outnumbered the ones that tried to pull one over on this young officer.

TWENTY-ONE

I rECEIVED ONLY ONE FITNESS REPORT DURING THIS TOUR. Captain Alexander provided Captain O'Donnell's input for this report. Captain O'Donnell showed me that he had given me an all "A" fitness report with a stellar written narrative to support the A report. He forwarded it to the Surgeon General's Chief of Staff, another MSC captain. The next day Captain O'Donnell told me that my fitness report was ready to be signed and that I should go see the Chief of Staff and sign it. Well when I got there I noticed that one of the A grades had been changed to a B. I was not about to argue with this captain so I signed it and went back to see Captain O'Donnell. He asked me if I was happy and I indicated that I was but that I noticed that one of the A marks he had given me was changed to a B. He asked me for the report. When he reviewed it he got up from his desk and said, "Come with me."

We went to see the Chief of Staff and Captain O'Donnell asked him if he knew me. The Chief of Staff said that he had just met me. Captain O'Donnell, in a forceful voice said, "If you don't know him how the hell can you change one of my evaluations marks?" The Chief of Staff said that no ensign was an all A officer. Captain O'Donnell said, "This one is and you will change his mark back to an A or we will discuss this with the Surgeon General." I could see that Captain O'Donnell was going to get his way, but I also knew that I had just pissed off another senior Medical Department officer.

It was coming up on transfer time again and I asked Captain O'Donnell if it wasn't time for me to go to a hospital for duty. After a minute's thought he asked if I had a Bachelor's Degree. When I said no, he said he thought I needed to go to the George Washington University here in D.C. and get a degree in Healthcare Administration. How could I argue with this logic, the Navy was paying? So, off to George Washington University I went.

My second shot at college and I found this one not only challenging, but I enjoyed the course of study. I graduated with a solid B+ average.

As graduation time approached I called my detailer and was very gruffly told to call Captain O'Donnell since he was my detailer. I was stunned. I called Captain O'Donnell and told him what had happened and he just laughed. I asked him if I would ever get off of the detailers' bad list. He said, "Don't worry, they change every two years."

I finally asked him what was going to happen to me. He said that I was going to the Enlisted Personnel Management Center (EPMAC) in New Orleans to work for another of his old shipmates. I felt myself falling into a career path that may not be such a good one, especially with all the hospital personnel officer billets disappearing.

Wanda and I packed up the kids and headed south to New Orleans. Captain O'Donnell's friend was Captain Davis. He was a great boss and pretty much left me alone with my staff of one master chief petty officer and two first class petty officers. To be honest, the Master Chief pretty much ran the show and this gave me time to really get to understand the enlisted personnel system in the Navy. It also gave me time to work on my Master of Arts Degree in Human Resources Management, which I finished during this tour.

Captain Davis retired and was replaced by Captain Franklin. As luck would have it Captain Franklin had been Wanda's immediate boss at U.S. Atlantic Fleet when I was at ServLant. He even was still using the coffee mug that Wanda had given him when he transferred from Atlantic Fleet. He showed it to me and asked if I remembered it. How could I forget? It had his name on it and the Marine Corps Anchor and Globe versus the Navy Device.

Captain Franklin was another great boss. Near the end of my tour he called me to his office and asked me if I would take another job working for him vice transferring out. Of course I couldn't say no, but I was curious about the job.

The job was to be the OIC of the Navy's Transient Monitoring Unit (TMU). I would have a staff of fifteen working for me, the junior of which were two second class petty officers, and the senior was a master chief. Plus I had my own secretary. All enlisted members were handpicked for assignment to TMU. They were all personnelmen. While Captain Franklin was my immediate boss, the unit fell under the BuPers Personnel Shop or Pers-3. All of the officer and enlisted detailers worked for Pers-3. I had to go for an interview with a two-star admiral, also called a rear admiral (RADM) at Pers-3 and if he deemed me acceptable he would direct my orders be issued. I was acceptable because of my extensive personnel background and the previous OICs of TMU were unable to crack the patient system at the hospitals. The hospitals had successfully fended off all efforts of TMU to keep the patient pipeline clean. So going in I knew that in addition to all the other transient facilities, my job was to fix the patient transient system, which was seriously broken. This was my second opportunity to upset another large section of the Medical Service Corps.

The main job for TMU was to travel Navy-wide to all transient units, brigs, schools, and hospitals to ensure that the transients there were being managed properly and were promptly returned to a "full for duty" status as soon as possible.

This was a two year assignment and I was on the road almost every week. Frequently I would leave on Monday, return on Friday, only to leave again the following Monday.

We re-wrote the medical portion of the Navy's *Enlisted Transfer Personnel Manual* during this tour and got it approved. As a result of mismanagement of transients we were directly responsible for two COs of two large shore-based facilities being relieved of their command. All in all the tour was a great experience and TMU received a letter of appreciation from the Secretary of the Navy for our efforts during my tour. I received the first of five Meritorious Service Medals at the end of my tour.

****

Our next tour was both disappointing and fun. Fun, because we were going home to Pensacola for duty; disappointing, because it was another personnel assignment. I was ordered to be the OIC of the Personnel Support Detachment (PSD) at Corry Field in Pensacola. This was basically the same office where Wanda and I had met! I was relieving Commander Ben Evers who became one of my best friends and one who later would save my career. He was going to BuPers to be the Medical Service Corps detailer.

Wanda quickly got a civil service job and got into a training program at the civilian personnel office that would eventually lead to her being a GS-11.

The PASS program was up and running well by this time and the PSDs were consolidated personnel offices on a single base. All PSDs were subordinate to a Personnel Support Activity (PSA). The PSA was the parent organizations that provided support and oversight to all the PSDs in a specific geographical area.

During this tour I was promoted to lieutenant commander (LCDR).

****

In the second year of my assignment I was really having a problem with my boss, Commander Manning, the CO of the PSA. While he was married, he was having an affair with a female first class petty officer that worked for me in my PSD. He was continuously giving me directions on what she would or would not do based upon what she wanted to do or not do.

The back breaker was when he had a trip planned and at the last minute decided that the first class petty officer needed to go on the trip with him. Well as luck would have it, she had the duty over the weekend that they would be gone. When I explained this to him he said, "She is going; the duty is your problem."

I could not resist it, I asked, "Is there something personal going on between you two?" He told me it was none of my damn business and that since I worked for him I would do as I was told. Again, I should have kept my mouth shut, but I said, "What do I tell the poor sap that has to stand her duty?" He screamed at me to just shut up and do as he said or he would relieve me as the OIC. The situation had gotten out of hand. I stood to attention and told him that he did not have to relieve me because I was quitting, and I grabbed my hat and left the building.

I went home and called Commander Evers and explained what had happened and made no excuse for my behavior. Fortunately for me Commander Evers had a history of problems with my CO when he was the XO at the PSA. I did not know that he had fleeted up to the CO's job when his boss had retired.

I had been promoted to LCDR during this tour and things were not looking good for further advancement.

Commander Evers remembered that I had been the OIC of the TMU in New Orleans. He asked me that if in my travels had I ever met a LCDR by the name of Dan Bowers. I said I knew him well when he was in charge of the transient facility at Great Lakes, Illinois. Commander Evers informed me that Dan was now a commander and worked for the Chief of Naval Education and Training (CNET). CNET was a vice admiral and the senior officer in the Pensacola area. The PSA and the subordinate PSDs all came under his authority. Commander Evers told me that he was going to call Commander Bowers and give him a heads up that I was on my way to see him. He said he would give him a little of the history of what was going on so that I did not blindside him.

When I met with Commander Bowers, he was just as nice as could be. He asked if I minded if he invited the CNET Chief of Staff to join us. Of course I did not object, I told him. The Chief of Staff was a captain and I told him everything that had transpired and the history of Commander Manning's interference in the PSD involving the female first class petty officer.

The Chief of Staff directed Commander Bowers to go immediately to the PSD at Corry Station and talk to the senior enlisted member at the PSD and to see what he could find out about all of this.

Well as luck would have it Commander Manning and the first class petty officer had already left on their trip (a day early).

When we met the following morning with the Chief of Staff, Commander Bowers not only corroborated what I had said, but he said that the Senior Chief had told him that Commander Manning had contacted him directly on a number of occasions to get the Senior Chief to try and influence me with regards to the petty officer's evaluations and her internal work assignments in the PSD. Commander Bowers also spoke with several of the senior enlisted and two of the civilian workers and without exception they gave further examples of Commander Manning consorting with other female enlisted.

The Chief of Staff took Commander Bowers's investigation along with my statement to see the vice admiral. After reviewing the information the vice admiral directed the Chief of Staff to find Commander Manning wherever he was and to have him report to CNET as soon as possible.

I did not know where Commander Manning was but the Chief of Staff had to tell him that he was being relieved of his command in order to get his attention and get him on the road back to Pensacola.

Commander Manning was relieved of his command as a result of Admiral's Mast. This is just short of a Summary Courts Martial. At the Admiral's Mast I was sitting across the long table from Commander Manning. He did not look me in the eye during the entire proceeding. The vice admiral asked Commander Manning several questions based upon the information that Commander Bowers had provided and my statement. Commander Manning did not deny a single charge. The vice admiral asked me point blank: "Given an opportunity, would you work for this officer again?" My response was, "Only if the Navy ordered me to, but I certainly would prefer not to ever see him again much less work for him." Not only was Commander Manning relieved of his command, he was a frocked commander (promoted in all respects except for legal authority and pay) and the vice admiral rescinded his impending promotion and was told he was to submit his retirement papers as an LCDR.

Commander Bowers took me to his office after the Mast was completed and told me to take a seat in his chair and call Commander Evers. I did so and Commander Evers was quite pleased to hear that Commander Manning was relieved of his command. Commander Evers indicated that he was not going to leave me at the PSD and that BuPers had already order a line officer into the billet. I was the last Medical Service Corps personnel officer to run a Navy personnel office.

Commander Evers ordered me to be the administrative officer at the Naval Aerospace Medical Research Laboratory (NAMRL) in Pensacola. I thanked him and God that I finally was going to a medical facility after over nine years commissioned service.

TWENTY-TWO

T HE TOUR AS THE ADMIN OFFICER WAS INTERESTING and rewarding. In spite of everything that had happened to me and the assignments that I had been to, all my fitness reports were at the top of the list. Where I competed with other officers of my rank I was always ranked number one. All of this had gotten me promoted to LCDR.

One thing that made this tour not only interesting, but challenging was the financial part. I had a young Navy lieutenant, Sidney Hathcock, as my comptroller. The Navy works on a budget system of finances, but research labs work on an "overhead accounting" system of finance. In other words, the scientists have to sell their research projects and receive funding to conduct their research. These monies mostly come from other military organizations that provided the monies from their operating budget. But some actually came from civilian sources, mostly universities. Out of these monies comes an "overhead cost" to operate the facility. My job and the comptroller's job were not directly involved with research, but we were needed to support their efforts, so they had to account for our salaries and other costs in their research accounting. This type of fiscal accounting is common in private industry, but unique in the military. Thank God for Sidney. He had to quickly learn how this system worked, and he mastered it in a way that even amazed the scientists.

Almost as interesting during this tour was the opportunity to see many of the early training devices that were used in training the first group of astronauts. For example, the first true 360-degree motion picture theater was developed at NAMRL as well as a number of other fascinating machines and devices to help train astronauts. It was also at this facility where the first group of astronauts received their training.

A wonderful thing happened during this tour; I received permission from Jamie's natural father to adopt Jamie. He never spent much time with her after our initial departure from Pensacola and I think he was relieved that he would no longer have to pay child support, even though he was almost a year behind in payments. When we went to court and the judge explained to Jamie that this meant that she no longer would be the daughter of her natural father, but would be my daughter, she smiled and said, "That will make me so happy." Jamie and I have celebrated this day, July 5th, as a second birthday for both of us.

****

After two years, as I was approaching my projected rotation date at the research laboratory, I received a phone call from my detailer.

I learned that Commander Evers was no longer in that job. The new detailer was Commander Bruce Russel. I did not know it at the time but our paths would cross again and we would become good friends. Commander Russel had called to inform me that I had been selected to attend the Armed Forces Staff College in Norfolk, Virginia. The course that I would be taking would last for six months and I would be studying and learning how to work with Joint and Combined Staffs. Joint Staffs are when two or more U.S. services are working together. Combined Staffs are U.S. military and another country's military working together. The course of instructions was to prepare me to work on staffs that had all services and/or foreign personnel assigned. We were also taught how to develop War Plans using the Deliberate Planning Process. These included Operational Plans as well as Conceptual Plans

I asked where I was going after the course was over and he asked me where I would like to go. This was a new twist. Wanda had joined me on one of my TMU trips to Hawaii and later said that if we ever got the chance she wanted to do a tour there. So I took a chance with Commander Russel and after a few minutes he told me he had a billet that would be available in Hawaii when I graduated and he penciled me in.

As it turned out Commander Russel received an edict from the Chief of Naval Operations that all graduates from the Armed Forces Staff

College would be assigned to joint billets only. Commander Russel had planned to send me to the Medical Clinics Command at Pearl Harbor, but this new requirement cancelled those plans. Being the creative assignment officer that he was, he found a billet that reported to the CO of the Clinics Command but was the Navy liaison officer at Tripler Army Hospital, Honolulu.

By this time Wanda was accustomed to me coming home from work with news that something else crazy was happening to the Sullivan family. She was shocked and excited about the school and the prospect of going to Hawaii. After talking we decided that she, Jamie and Jean would stay in Pensacola until I had finished my school course and then we could all pack up and go to Hawaii from Norfolk after my graduation.

****

During my time in Norfolk I reached out to my good friend Ralph. I was devastated when I found him in the hospital with terminal cancer. After my six month school tour Ralph was still hanging on when we left Norfolk for Hawaii. I knew that I had seen him for the last time.

****

Being the seasoned champ that she was, Wanda sold the house and rented a small apartment so that when it was time to go we could just meet up at my graduation.

Dee was on her own by this time, but she came to my graduation. Wanda, Jamie and Jean arrived and I knew that something was wrong. Wanda explained that Jamie and Jean were not excited at all about going to Hawaii. Jamie was attending junior college in Pensacola and was old enough to just say no, but we acted as if she had no choice; she was going where we were going. Jean was finishing her sophomore year at Tate High School and was a member of the school's Color Guard. Both had boyfriends and other anchors to Pensacola. But after some lengthy discussions, both finally came with us to Hawaii.

****

While we were awaiting on-base housing we were staying in the Hale

Koa Military Hotel on Waikiki Beach. The location was the best on Waikiki Beach and right next door to the Hilton Hotel where Don Ho performed every night.

The Navy was paying for us to stay in the Hale Koa and we were there for six weeks before base housing became available.

By the time we left the hotel, Jamie was enrolled at the University of Hawaii and Jean was going to one of the few high schools that had a band with a color guard. We were able to get an exception for her to attend the school outside of her district because of the color guard. She was much more advanced in her color guard skills than her classmates and was selected to be the captain of the Color Guard.

I had reported to the CO of the Navy Medical Clinics Command and he had assigned me as the patient administration officer. This was quite a letdown for a LCDR. This is a billet that would normally be filled with a LTJG or perhaps a LT. I didn't have much choice because the CO had a senior chief petty officer doing the job at Tripler Army Hospital.

Wanda was fortunate that she got a civil service job before we moved out of the hotel. During the tour she took two or three transfers and eventually was back to her GS-11 pay grade.

The senior administrative Medical Service Corps officer was the Director for Administration (DFA) and he provided oversight to all the Command's administrative departments. Henry was a likable fellow, but it was obvious to me that he was not up to this job. He was a former food service officer who had previously managed an officer's club.

It did not take the CO and the XO long after my arrival to make the decision to move Henry to one of the five clinics the command managed. Henry would be the OIC of the clinic. The CO assigned me the job of DFA.

****

While we were getting settled in, I was invited to join a poker party involving several members of the command. This was a friendly, low stakes game and I truly enjoyed it and the company. When I came home that night Wanda broke the news to me that my friend Ralph had passed away. She said that she started to call me at the poker game but thought that Ralph would have appreciated her waiting until the game was over.

Another important person in my life was gone, but he will live forever in my memories.

****

Jamie was doing well at the University of Hawaii, Jean was doing well in her high school, Wanda had a good job and I was happier than I could ever remember. We actually were saving quite a bit of money living in government quarters and using the Military Commissary and Post Exchange.

During this tour Wanda and I, sometimes with both Jamie and Jean, and sometimes only with Jean, were able to travel quite a bit. We went to Hong Kong, Taiwan, Bangkok, Singapore, Malaysia, Communist China, Macaw and Japan. Life was great!

Jamie met a good looking young man and while I had my reservations about him there was no stopping her. Within several months they were married. Jamie continued at the University of Hawaii and got her BA degree in Communications.

That left us with only Jean still at home.

****

All good things must come to an end, however, and during my second year as DFA I received a phone call from a commander assigned to BuMed. He informed me that the Navy Component (NavCent) of the U.S. Central Command (CinCent), headquartered in Tampa, Florida, was in need of a medical planner. It just so happens that the NavCent was located in the Commander, U.S. Navy Pacific Fleet headquarters building in Hawaii. The BuMed commander indicated that I possessed the requisite skill because of my course of instruction at the Armed Forces Staff College. Bottom line was there was no one else anywhere near Hawaii to send to the job. He informed me that I had an appointment with Rear Admiral (RADM) Benson, the commander of NavCent, that afternoon at 1400.

When I got off of the phone I went to the CO's office and informed him of the phone call. He immediately called BuMed to protest. After being shifted to several different offices he spoke with the Surgeon

General's Chief of Staff and was informed that the decision was made and that if the RADM wanted me I was going to be transferred. The CO was not happy and I was not sure that I was either. I liked my current job. But, like a good sailor I was at NavCent at 1400 for my appointment.

Rear Admiral Benson was a big Irishman with snow white hair. His first question to me was, "If I decide to accept you as my medical planner where will your loyalties be, with me or with Navy medicine?"

I asked him, "Who will be signing my fitness reports?" He indicated that he would and I assured him that if that was the case then he had my complete loyalty.

We talked a little about the job and the fact that our Area of Responsibility (AOR) was the Middle East and North Africa. I had never been to that part of the world. After about twenty minutes or so he excused me and said that BuMed would be contacting me with his decision.

When I returned to my command, the CO indicated that BuMed wanted me to call them right away. I called and the commander that I had been dealing with indicated that RADM Benson had accepted me and that I would receive order within the next twenty-four hours to report within two days. My CO was not happy; however, he did not blame me as he knew that I had not initiated this. He gave me a glowing transfer fitness report and wanted to give me a Meritorious Service Medal. I already had two and asked him to drop the award down to the Navy Commendation Medal since I did not have one. He laughed and said okay.

I detached Navy Medical Clinics Command, Hawaii, on Friday and reported to NavCent on Monday morning.

After a quick acquaintance meeting with the Chief of Staff and my department head, Ryan Miller, I was told that the admiral wanted to see me.

I reported to him and I could see that something serious was about to be discussed. He filled me in on the only U.S. military base in the Middle East: The Administrative Support Unit (ASU) in Bahrain. The base consisted of about five acres and had a staff of about 200 military and civilians. The military members were allowed to bring their dependents with them and that raised the U.S. population in the area, not counting the embassy, to near 400. There was an American run school for dependents near the ASU that was also under NavCent. It was a Department of Defense school and it provided boarding for a number of students. United States embassy personnel throughout the Middle East sent their school-age children to this school where they were boarded during the school year. There were also numerous dependent students of royal families from throughout the Middle Eastern countries attending the school.

There was a small medical clinic on the base that had very limited capabilities. Most of the U.S. patients found themselves being treated at one of several Bahraini hospitals. The reviews from these hospitals were mixed. The dependents by and large were not happy with the care provided by the local hospitals.

Rear Admiral Benson indicated that my first order of business was to go to Bahrain and determine the minimal staff and capabilities the clinic needed to provide good basic support to the U.S. citizens eligible for care. He then dropped the bombshell; I was to leave the next day and "don't come back until you have a completed study."

I went back to my department head and he said, "Not what you expected, was it?" He told me that the comptroller had my Temporary Duty Orders (TAD) and plane tickets to Bahrain. The return trip was open ended.

Before I could do anything I had to be issued my Desert Cammie Uniforms. That was the uniform of the day for us in Hawaii and when on duty in the AOR. This took about two hours and to my surprise they were able to sew my name tag on the right side of all my shirts and U.S. Navy on the left. The uniform issue guy said that I could take everything home with me then and to come back within two hours and they would have my uniforms washed and pressed.

I went home to pack and I called Wanda at work and broke the news to her. While shocked at first she as usual took the news in stride. She asked her boss if she could take the rest of the day off to assist me and he was most accommodating.

Wanda kept her chin up and assured me that she could handle things until I returned. I was not sure, but felt there must be some means of communication from Bahrain to NavCent; if so I was sure we would get a chance to talk and I would keep her informed as to when I might be headed back home.

My flight was not until 1600 the following day so it gave me some additional time to collect information about Bahrain and the cultures of the Middle East.

I was told that since I was traveling across more than five time zones I could remain overnight (RON) at a country of my choosing, or I could opt to fly business class and fly straight through. I found that no U.S. airlines flew to Bahrain, therefore I would have to change to a foreign airline somewhere along the way.

I also found out that when I traveled on a foreign airline I was entitled to travel business class at no additional charge to the government. So what that meant was that I suffered in coach to the first overseas destination, got a room for the night and then flew on to Bahrain business class. The best of both worlds.

TWENTY THREE

WHEN I ARRIVED IN BAHRAIN THE CLINIC PHYSICIAN, an LCDR, and a civilian employee met me at the airport. I realized right away the civilian employee's importance as he walked me through immigration and customs without as much as a "Welcome to Bahrain." I got to like the civilian, named Homsa, and made use of his skills, knowledge and connections in a number of meetings with the local officials. Homsa was Iranian by birth but had lived in Bahrain almost all of his life.

The doctor had made reservations for me in the Gulf Hotel, a five-star accommodation. The luxury was unbelievable. I asked him about the expense and he said it was below my quarter's allowance and that all hotels in Bahrain were five stars, with the exception of some flophouses that locals used.

I was jet-lagged, but ready to go to work until I saw my hotel room. He suggested that I relax, get a good night's sleep and he would meet me for breakfast in the morning. The breakfast buffet was unbelievable. Everything but pork, but the beef bacon was a creditable substitute.

When I met with the clinic physician he informed me that he had made an appointment for me and him to meet with the senior military medical officer, basically, the Surgeon General of the Bahraini Military. When we got to the Surgeon General's office I found out that he was a member of the royal family. He and his brother, another physician, were quite pleasant and seemed pleased to have me join them.

We were served dates and buttermilk. I happen to like buttermilk, but I am not high on dates; but these were quite delicious. I noticed the clinic physician trying to give me some sort of sign but I was not sure what he was trying to convey. I found out shortly that he was trying to warn me not to fill up on the buttermilk and dates. When these dishes were removed a parade of servers came into the dining room and they had tray after tray of food. I did not know what to say. It all looked so good but I was full from the dates and buttermilk. I forced myself to eat much more than I thought possible. The last thing I wanted to do was offend them. I was almost sick when we departed.

The Surgeon General made a point of letting me know that the family had a private beach and only family members and members of the U.S. Military were allowed on it. They said that they hoped to see me at the beach at some point during my visit. Overall, I found the Arabs whom I met to be very polite and courteous to a fault.

I spent the next two and one half weeks reviewing the clinic facility and staff, the daily patient workload and the referrals to local civilian facilities. I visited all of the Bahraini hospitals and specialty clinics that we referred our patients to and determined that we should be able to do more in house in our ASU Clinic. All we needed to take better care of our patients were a few more staff and the ability to do basic laboratory work and take x-rays. I worked up a position paper indicating what was needed. I showed the paper to the senior physician at the clinic and he was delighted. But he was also practical, he told me that they had submitted repeated request for some of the improvements that I had identified and that none was ever approved.

****

When I got back to Hawaii and reported to RADM Benson with my report, he read it and then reached into his desk drawer and handed me a similar study that had been done by a Navy physician captain. There was one more billet required in his study than in mine, everything else was almost identical. I was confused. Rear Admiral Benson said that he had asked BuMed to send an expert out to Bahrain to do basically the same thing that I had done. When the captain filed his report, BuMed said he was basically "nuts." Although the RADM said he reminded BuMed that the captain was *their* expert, they still maintained that his study was not accurate.

Rear Admiral Benson left for Washington, D.C. the following morning with both reports. He went to the Chief of Naval Operations (CNO) N-2

(Personnel) with the two reports and requested assistance. Once again I was between the big boys at BuMed and a senior line officer. CNO J-2 ordered BuMed to identify the billets to be transferred to NavCent that I had identified in my study. The fight was over; the Bahrain clinic belonged to NavCent, not BuMed. The J-2 was able to get the funds to make the needed changes to the clinic and within four months all the new bodies were assigned to the clinic and all of the renovations to support a small lab and an x-ray facility were in place.

When RADM Benson returned he was one happy man. He had done what needed to be done to support his people in Bahrain. The morale of the staff and dependents rose immediately after the changes were put in place.

TWENTY-FOUR

I SETTLED IN AND BEGAN WORKING ON SEVERAL operational plans and conceptual plans. The big plan at the minute was a scenario where the USSR would invade Iran and take over their oil fields.

Medical planning was not easy in that we used a system called WMMICS, which had been designed to help the war-fighters and the logisticians develop the load planning of all ships and aircraft needed to support a specific plan. Someone had written a medical planning module and made it a part of the system. The medical planning module was not user friendly and tended to lose data and/or merge information from different parts of the system. I also found out that while I did not do the Marine Medical Planning they submitted their tape to me for me to merge with my Navy Medical Plan. The Marine planner had no idea what she was doing and it took me going to Camp Pendleton several times to get their plan where I could use the information in my plan.

One memorable trip that RADM Benson and five members of his staff, including me, made was to U. S. Central Command (CentCom) in Tampa, Florida, to brief the Commander in Chief (CinC) on the Navy's portion of the current Operational Plan that CentCom was working on.

It was memorable because the current CinC was a four-star Marine general who was notorious for firing members of his staff if he did not approve of their performance. When he fired a staff member they were not allowed back into the headquarters building. They stayed in a building out back until their orders were received and they could leave the area.

We started our brief with the "Intelligence Brief." About five minutes into the brief the Marine general stopped the briefer and told him that he did not know what he was talking about and dismissed him from the briefing room. I thought, oh heck this is going to be interesting.

There were three more briefers before me and he summarily dismissed each of them much the same as he had dismissed the Intelligence Officer. I was the only briefer that was not kicked out of the briefing. That was because before I got to brief the general he'd had enough. He turned to RADM Benson and said, "You need to take your staff back to Hawaii and do a heck of a lot of work on this plan before you make another effort to present your plan to me." Rear Admiral Benson replied, "Yes, Sir." And we departed for the airport to go home two days earlier than we had planned.

I don't know what impact this had on RADM Benson's career, but I felt that we had somehow let him down.

Later that year the promotion to his second star did not occur as we had hoped. Rear Admiral Benson showed more class than I thought I would ever be able to do. He knew that we were disappointed that he was not promoted. He called the entire staff together-- officers, enlisted and civilians. He said that he knew that we were disappointed in his failure to get promoted, but he pointed out that all of us would face that eventually if we stayed in the Navy long enough. Not every officer can expect to retire as a four-star. He thanked us for our support and said that we had nothing to do with his not being promoted.

I found out later that he was only the second helicopter pilot to ever be promoted to RADM. And the other one also retired as a one-star. I guess helicopter pilots were not respected in the aviation community as much as the fixed-wing pilots.

****

All in all the tour was interesting and I made several more trips to the Middle East. Rear Admiral Benson and I became friends, as friendly as an LCDR and a rear admiral can become anyway. His tour was coming to an end and we were sorry to see him go.

After the change of command we had a new commander, RADM Fellows. He was a nice enough guy but did not have Benson's personality.

About this time we also had a change of command at our parent headquarters, U. S. Central Command, in Tampa. An Army four star general named Davis took command and immediately changed the focus of our planning from the Soviet Union attacking Iran to Iraq attacking Kuwait and Saudi Arabia to obtain their oil fields.

The new general also decided against the annual CentCom exercise, "Bright Star," where all of the CentCom components met in Egypt to play war games in the desert. The general brought all of the component staffs to a Command Post Exercise (CPX) at Hurlburt Field in the panhandle of Florida. He said that he knew his component commanders knew how to fight, but he was more concerned about their ability to communicate among themselves if we had to go to war.

Rear Admiral Fellows took the principle planers for NavCent staff to the exercise. The exercise was in late July 1990 and the Operational Plan we were to exercise was OPlan 1002-90, the invasion of Kuwait by Iraq.

On the way to Hurlburt Field I picked up a magazine on the plane that had an extensive article about a Russian hospital ship that was cruising the world performing laser eye surgery. It was very well written article and I enjoyed reading about the ship.

Once all the components were all established in Hurlburt and the exercise started via a computer program, General Davis began to visit each of the components and met with the staffs of each component commander. When he was introduced to me he took my hand into his massive paw and asked, "So, Doc, tell me what you know about this Russian hospital ship that is running a goodwill tour all over the place?" Hell, I was an expert; I had just read a ten page article about the ship. He seemed to be impressed that I was knowledgeable about the ship and what it was accomplishing. In the next year or so I had several occasions to run into the General and he always smiled and asked how things were going with me. I'm sure he did much the same with any number of junior officers in his command, but the fact that he remembered me was impressive.

As the exercise progressed it got confusing because we had to work our real world issues as well as the exercise. On about day three of the exercise we started receiving real world message traffic that looked like day one of the exercise traffic. We were assured that this was real world message traffic. By the time the exercise was over and we were getting ready to go back to Hawaii the real world message traffic was up to about day four of our exercise messages. I could see the concern on the faces of the senior officers.

We returned home to Hawaii on the August 1, 1990 and RADM Fellows told us to take the following day off.

I was usually one of the first to come to work each day, but when I arrived to work after the day off, the Chief of Staff, the Intelligence Officer, the Operations Officer and my boss, the Logistics Officer, were all there and in with RADM Fellows.

I knew that something serious was going on. I asked the comptroller what she knew and she said that Iraq had invaded Kuwait the previous day. The NavCent staff consisted of twelve officers and about eighteen enlisted. We were the equivalent of a fleet commander who had a staff of hundreds, but in actuality we were primarily a planning staff with fleet authority and responsibility.

Though I was not one of the junior officers, I did not normally get invited into the RADM's office for high level meetings. However, as I sat at my desk, RADM Fellows's AID came in and said that the admiral wanted to see me ASAP.

I was impressed with the group in his office. All were department heads except me. Rear Admiral Fellows asked if I had been briefed on the current situation. I told him that all I had heard was that Iraq had invaded Kuwait. He said that was true. He said that indications were that we would be moving our headquarters to Bahrain. The decision had been made that I had as much if not more knowledge of ASU Bahrain and the area as anyone on the staff. So, he said he was sending me forward to help get some sort of headquarters established. He indicated that I should anticipate our staff growing so to think about where we could locate. He said that the comptroller would be cutting my orders and making plane reservations. I asked if it were possible for me to take a couple of other Navy Medical Department personnel with me. He said if I could get Navy Medicine to provide me support he would support whatever I thought I needed. I thought, "Holy Hell, a blank check!"

Though we were several time zones ahead of the Washington, D.C.

area the folks at BuMed were at work and already calling me. When I called them back a captain asked if I could provide him a copy of the OPlan and what Navy medical support was anticipated. I explained to him that there was no completed OPlan, only a draft and I was not authorized to give it out. I also explained that I was leaving later in the day as the advance party from NavCent Headquarters. I told him that I was going to need some additional medical personnel to go with me. He said that should not present a problem, and asked if I had anyone in mind. I told him that there was a young ensign at the Pearl Harbor Clinics Command that I would like to take to help with the heavy lifting. I also told him that I would need a senior enlisted member, preferably a master chief petty officer. He told me to provide him the ensign's name and he would take care of his orders, and he told me that he had the perfect master chief on the BuMed staff that would be willing to go. He said, he had to ask if I could come through Washington and brief the BuMed staff and the Surgeon General on what I could share with them. I got permission from the Chief of Staff to go through Washington and he said I could share anything I had with them.

I called Wanda at work and once again broke the news to her that I was on my way to the Middle East, today. She said she would meet me at home to help me get packed. I was pretty much packed from the exercise so it did not take much.

While I was taking care of things in the office, message orders for Ensign Brown arrived and within fifteen minutes Ensign Brown himself arrived. He was out of breath and obviously confused. I explained to him that we were on our way to the Middle East and that the NavCent supply clerk would issue him his Desert cammies and other articles he needed to take with him, including a gas mask. He was instructed in how to put the gas mask on and told to take all his stuff home and pack it in one of the canvas bags provided as a substitute for a suitcase. He was at the point of tears. I put my arm around his shoulder and assured him that things would be okay

He did not share with me that his bride to be had just arrived from New York the previous day. Wanda found out about his fiance and took her under her wing for the duration of our deployment.

****

We left out of Hawaii on a late flight that would get us into Washington at about the beginning of the work day, except the day was Saturday the 4th of August. To my surprise there was a commander waiting for us at the airport and he took us straight to BuMed. When we arrived he took us to the Surgeon General's conference room where at least twenty captains and one- and two-star RADMs were waiting. I briefed the Surgeon General and his staff on all that I had and they were somewhat taken aback when I told them that Navy-wise we were taking both hospital ships, the *Mercy* and the *Comfort*, as well as three fleet hospitals. One of the one-star RADMs looked at me and said, "You realize that this will strip every one of our Stateside hospitals of their staff." The Surgeon General looked at him and said, "It may do so, but we have an obligation to support the fleet, especially during wartime."

The Surgeon General in a short private conversation assured me that we would have BuMed's complete support and asked if there was anything else he could do to help. I told him that sooner or later NavCent was going to need a fleet surgeon. He indicated that he had the right man in mind and to just let him know when we needed him. I thanked him and assured him that I would do everything I could to keep him and his staff informed as things progressed.

A very sharp looking master chief was waiting for me when I left the conference room. To my surprise he had been issued his desert cammies at Quantico the day before, so he was ready to travel.

The entire trip was filled with questions from Ensign Brown and the Master Chief about what they were to expect when they arrived in Bahrain. My main advice was to stay away from all women, don't drink too much and always treat all the Middle Easterners with politeness and respect. Dress conservatively, no shorts or tank top shirts. Otherwise enjoy the culture and the sites.

When we arrived at the airport in Bahrain, our trusted civilian employee, Hamsa, and the clinic physician were waiting for us. Once again Hamsa whisked us right through customs and immigration.

On the way to our hotel, once again the Gulf Hotel, things got exciting.

While driving down the main road along the gulf shore we started to receive heavy machine gun fire right across the front of our vehicle. The doctor was driving and he swerved off of the road and right into a ditch. We bailed out and hid behind the auto. Nothing else happened and soon the Bahraini police arrived. They assisted us in getting our vehicle back on the road and explained that the shooting was coming from a Kuwaiti gun boat that was firing on the local Iraqi embassy. We just happened to be in the wrong place at the wrong time.

When we arrived at the Gulf Hotel, the Master Chief commented that he thought he might enjoy this war. He and the ensign said they had never stayed in a hotel that nice in their lives. I told them to get settled in and place a wake-up call for 0500. We would meet at breakfast at 0600 and the clinic would have someone pick us up by 0645. Goodnight.

****

After breakfast and arriving at ASU Bahrain I met with the OIC. He had received notice that we were coming and what our task was to be. He suggested that we start setting the headquarters up in the recreation/library building as it was the largest building on the base. The entire contents of the building had already been removed. NavCent began as about thirty personnel and grew to over 125. Lucky for us the U.S. Embassy had just completed a new compound and later we were able to move into the old embassy after they departed

We went to survey the building. I had been in it several times before but did not realize how small it was, probably no more than 5,000 square feet. I had a list of things that the Chief of Staff had provided me, plus some additional things that I thought we would need. I started to dictate to Ensign Brown and the Master Chief the list of items we would need including at least three, hopefully four, warehouses in the 50,000–75,000 square foot range. As I dictated, the Master Chief wrote as fast as he could to keep up. The ensign just stood there in shock. After about fifteen minutes of spouting off the initial list I turned to go away. The ensign stopped me and asked, "Commander, how are we to get all of this stuff?" I told him, "Ensign Brown, I have my problems and you have yours." The Master Chief grabbed the ensign by the arm and led him away.

I was not surprised when I realized that the Master Chief had noted in our short conversation with the OIC that he had told me where the Navy's contracting officer was located on the base.

I went to the contracting officer's office and the Master Chief and the ensign were already there. They had someone helping them and I spent a few minutes with the contracting officer explaining that a lot of gear was in transit and that we would need a lot of warehouse space to off-load the maritime prepositioned ships that would be arriving within the next week or two. He took on the task.

****

On the 8th of August RADM Fellows and most of the remaining staff arrived. He seemed pleased with the effort we had made. He had his private office with an adjourning conference room that would accommodate twelve people at the beautiful conference table. We had established office space with both secure and non-secure phones for each of his department heads with limited space for their staffs.

About the time RADM Fellows arrived the Navy went crazy. They realized that all the Central Command Component commanders were three-star generals and the Navy Component commander was a one-star rear admiral. The first move was by CentCom when they designated a two-star RADM from the USS *Oak Ridge,* a joint command and control ship assigned permanently to the middle east, as NavCent. Their logic was that he was there and at least he was a little more senior. Meanwhile, the Chief of Naval Operations seeing the situation designated the two-star RADM at the embassy in Riyadh, Saudi Arabia, as NavCent. Now we had three NavCent commanders with message traffic going to each and none of them knowing what was going on.

****

Unlike my first experience in war, during the entire Gulf War I received mail or an audio tape every day from Wanda. Sometimes several would come the same day and I would look at the postmarks and read them in the order that she had sent them. When an audio tape came I would save it until my roommate had the duty or was not in the room and then I would listen to it. All communications from Wanda were upbeat and positive. I found out later that she had been dealing with a number of issues including Jean showing herself over a young Airman in the Air Force, whom she eventually married. I could not help but to think that all that time she needed me, but she took the burden on alone because she felt that I did not need the distractions. She was kind of cute when she found out that I was living in a five star hotel. I think that even knowing that, I was not living the life of Riley. It was amusing that we were running a war from five star hotels.

It was at this point that I got word that the Surgeon General had designated a physician captain as the NavCent Surgeon and that he was on his way to Bahrain. The new NavCent Surgeon was Captain Frank Deloach.

Two days later I received a call from Deloach requesting that I come to the airport and pick him up. The clinic doctor volunteered to go get him. After about an hour the clinic doctor called and said that he was not at the airport. A few minutes later Deloach called again and was somewhat irate that we had not picked him up. I explained that there was an LCDR physician at the airport looking for him. Well after some detective work we realized that Deloach was at the airport in Dhahran, Saudi Arabia, not in Bahrain.

It was well into the afternoon now and I knew that I would not be able to get across the twenty-seven-mile crossway that connected Bahrain to Saudi Arabia. The Saudi customs and immigration station on the crossway was known for holding people up for hours. I think it was more a show of authority than anything else.

I explained to the new surgeon that I would not be able to come and get him before tomorrow. He was not happy. He wanted to know where he was to sleep and I mentioned that a newly arrived Air Force medical evacuation unit was adjacent to the Saudi airport and suggested that he see if they could put him up for the night. I asked him to give me a call at 0800 tomorrow and I would have arrangements made to come and get him.

The ASU had a helicopter detachment that had three CH-53s and the associated aircrews and maintenance personnel. They were named "The

Desert Ducks." With the assistance of the Desert Ducks I was able to fetch Deloach the following morning.

He came into the office with his ass on his shoulders. He was complaining about how he had flown all night and half the next day to arrive, tired when he found that he was not even in the right country. What could I say?

Shortly after his arrival I found out that his top secret clearance had expired and that he was not going to be able to attend the morning and evening meetings or read over half of the message traffic that came in each day. His attitude went from bad to worse. Here I had a boss that was in charge but one with whom I could not communicate anything important. The Intel folks went to work immediately to get his clearance updated.

Three days later his clearance was approved and he was a little easier to get along with.

****

The commander U.S. 7th Fleet, aboard his flag ship the *Blue Ridge*, from Japan, was a vice admiral designated U.S. Navy CentCom commander. Since he was a three-star and equal to the other component commanders in rank some semblance of order came to the U.S. Navy in the Middle East.

The question of what to do with the original NavCent staff was settled quickly as RADM Fellows was designated the N-4, logistics commander for NavCent, and he and his staff would stay ashore and manage all logistic issues including all medical issues.

Additional confusion was brought with the 7th Fleet in that they had their own fleet surgeon, Captain Oliver, and their own medical planner, LCDR Phillip Hayes. Obviously when they arrived the 7th Fleet Surgeon reported to RADM Fellows as the new NavCent Surgeon. The 7th Fleet Surgeon was stunned when he found out that there was already a NavCent Surgeon onboard. When it was established that Captain Deloach was the senior of the two and therefore would remain the NavCent Surgeon, Captain Oliver initially decided to remain ashore and be Captain

Deloach's deputy. I was senior to LCDR Hayes so I remained in the senior medical admin position.

After a couple of days it was obvious that Captain Deloach and Captain Oliver were not going to be able to work together. Captain Oliver moved back aboard the *Blue Ridge* with the NavCent Headquarters staff. Lieutenant Commander Hayes decided that the action was going to be ashore so he requested permission to remain with the new NavCent N-4 organization. We had not heard the last of Captain Oliver.

Since ASU Bahrain was the only true U.S. military facility in the Middle East everyone began to ship stuff directly there. Absolute chaos. Every airplane that landed at the airport had additional Navy medical personnel aboard. I don't know who was making the decisions back in the States about what we needed but they were doing a fine job of screwing things up. We kept those that we thought we could use and sent the remainder back home.

At the Bahraini government's request, we requested that a Navy medical surgical team be assigned so that we could place them in one of the local Bahraini hospitals. They showed up and took to their new assignment like ducks to water. In fact after about three weeks I could not recognize most of them because they were not allowed to wear uniforms in the civilian hospital and they assimilated to the point where we had to bring the senior officer in and explain to him that his was still a military organization, in or out of uniform. He was to conduct himself appropriately and he was to ensure that his staff complied with Navy grooming standards.

****

There was so much material coming in via airplane that I assigned eight corpsmen to the airport to capture anything that appeared to be medical in nature. I did not care if it was Army, Navy, Air Force or Marine; I took charge of it and had it placed in one of the three warehouses we had contracted for medical equipment. An inventory, by service, was maintained because I knew that sooner or later someone was going to come looking for all of this stuff.

****

I never knew what was going to come to my desk each day. I was running on about five hours sleep a night. Though we had a designated fleet surgeon who went to all the staff meetings, RADM Fellows insisted that I also attend since I had written the medical portion of the OPlan and had been in on the ground floor. This did not make Captain Deloach happy, but I tried not to interject myself into any of the conversations unless specifically asked something.

In spite of the work schedule we had to maintain our military fitness. I would force drink water all morning so that when lunch time came and I went jogging I would not become dehydrated. I tried to drink at least four liters of water each morning. Running in 105–115 degree weather just made the water in your body pore out. I believe that I would actually lose as many as five to seven pounds running at lunch.

One morning I looked up and there was an Australian physician commander standing at my desk in search of injectable polio vaccine. I had never heard of injectable polio vaccine. I explained that we were inoculated with the vaccine on a sugar cube in grade school. He informed me that Australia did not inoculate their children because polio was not a problem in Australia, but that it was prevalent in the Middle East and he needed to protect his Australian service members. I got on the phone to BuMed with the problem and I don't know where they found it but they indicated it would be in Bahrain within forty-eight hours. The Australian doctor was happy and when it arrived; I gave all of it to him.

****

A huge shipment of a new antibody called Ciprofloxacin (Cipro) arrived and I told the Master Chief to place it in one of the warehouses. A few days later an Army physician colonel was at my desk demanding that I give the Cipro to him. I had received no guidance on the distribution of any of the medical materials I had been collecting and informed him that he would have to get someone to authorize me to give the Cipro to him. I did not know it at the time, but the Cipro was to be used in case Iraq used anthrax against our coalition forces. Eventually a message arrived from the CNO directing me to turn over all of the Cipro to the Army Component Surgeon.

This was becoming one screwed up war

****

Every large ship that entered the AOR with a captain medical corps aboard immediately tried to take charge of the entire theater's medical system. We were constantly drafting messages for the vice admiral to release back to the "I'm in charge medical officer's" line commander telling him to keep his medical officer under control and that all medical guidance would emanate from the NavCent N-4.

The first fleet hospital (Fleet Hospital 5) arrived in theater and was unable to off-load at the piers in Dhahran because of the backlog of ships trying to off load. It was estimated that it would be three weeks before it could be off-loaded. I recommended a solution and Captain Deloach agreed to have the fleet hospital off-loaded at Al Jebel, Saudi Arabia, a port about eighty miles north of Dhahran. We arranged to have flat-bed trucks available to truck the hospital back to the Dhahran area were the OPlan said it would be established.

Two days later I received a call from the captain in charge of erecting the fleet hospital and he told me that he had been directed to set the hospital up in Al Jebel. I was stunned. I asked who made that decision and he indicated that the CO of the ship with the advice of a Navy Medical Service Corps LCDR had made the decision. I said, "Stop, don't do anything." He said, "Too late, we've started to open the containers and putting this stuff back in was out of the question."

I drove up to Al Jebel to see what could be done. If things unfolded as was possible and Iraq moved into Saudi Arabia we would lose this hospital within the first forty-eight hours. But the big concern was a petrochemical plant that was upwind of the hospital and the prevailing winds that time of the year would bring deadly gases directly across the hospital's location. We had to hope that Iraq did not damage the petrochemical plant. I finally found the LCDR that had recommended the site and when I finished with him he knew that if any of the scenarios that I presented were to occur he would be responsible for the deaths of upwards of 1,200 medical and medical support personnel. It was too late to change things now so we started to develop evacuation plans for the hospital staff if it appeared Iraq was going to invade Saudi Arabia.

When I got back to my office in Bahrain there was an Army colonel doctor standing at my desk with an Army nurse and a master sergeant. The doctor said that he had been told by the Army Component medical planner to come see me about getting a 500-bed Army combat support hospital that had been prepositioned in a local warehouse. I thought, "You have got to be kidding me." I contacted Major Roberts, the ArCent medical planner, to see what was going on. He informed me that the combat support hospital was to be set up in Bahrain and that the staff was a reserve medical element and that the initial staff of personnel were expected in Bahrain within the next forty-eight hours. I asked how many people we were talking about. He indicated somewhere between 175 and 250. I asked where he planned to house them. He had no answer. I could see this mess getting out of hand quickly. I asked the colonel to have a seat and that I would be right back. I went to see Captain Deloach and he and I went to the Chief of Staff. The Chief of Staff decided the RADM needed to be informed. When we shared the situation with him he called the G-4 at ArCent and asked what the hell was going on. The G-4 had no answers but said that he had no one he could send from Saudi Arabia to Bahrain to deal with the issue. He gave us a contract number to use and asked us to do what we could to help these people.

I had Ensign Brown take the colonel and his staff to the Gulf Hotel and get them settled while I gave this some thought.

Captain Deloach did not want any part of solving this problem and I did not know where to start. I called Major Roberts at ArCent and asked where the hospital was to be located. He said that according to his plan it was to be at Sheikh Isa Air Base. Sheikh Isa Air Base was supposed to be a secret, but that was no longer the case.

I contacted my contact at the American embassy and talked to him about this. He asked me to give him some time to talk to the commander at Sheikh Isa Air Base and see what he thought.

The embassy guy called me back about three hours later and said that he and I had an appointment with the commander of the base at 0900 the following day. He also said, "Oh, by the way, he is not a happy camper."

We were there the following morning and the commander was very cordial and after the routine hot tea and dates he summoned his driver and we went for a ride around the base. I identified several locations that were big enough and on solid ground, but he had an excuse as to why none was available. Eventually we found ourselves near the beach. I explained that this location had several drawbacks including it was almost three miles from the nearest building on the main base. He basically said take it or leave it.

I returned to my headquarters after dropping off the embassy guy and called Major Roberts and explained the situation. He said that if that was the only place offered then to tell the Army colonel who was to be the CO that was where the hospital was to be established. Major Roberts asked if I had an Army contract number. I assured him that I did and he requested that I contract some flatbed trucks to deliver the hospital to Sheikh Isa Air Base. When I shared this with the colonel, he was not pleased. He did not know it, but things were about to get worse.

The next afternoon I got a call from the civilian airport informing me that there were approximately 200 soldiers at the airport requesting transportation to somewhere. I called the contracting office and had ten buses dispatched to the airport with guidance to deliver these folks to the colonel at Sheikh Isa Air Base.

They arrived around midnight and I had just laid my head on my pillow when the phone rang. It was the American Embassy. The CO of Sheikh Isa Air Base was upset and wanted someone to come down there and deal with the mess. I asked the man from the embassy if he would request the Army's CO of the hospital to deal with it. I guess that is what happened because I did not hear anything else that night.

The following morning I decided I needed to go to Sheikh Isa and see what was going on. I was flabbergasted with what I found. The flatbed trucks were still sitting on the road fully loaded after three days. There were approximately eight tents erected. I found the hospital commander and asked what was going on. He said that his medical staff had never been trained in erecting the hospital. They had just gotten lucky and had found tents among the crates on the trucks and had pushed them off the trucks and busted them open and had set up the tents that I saw. Most of the 250 personnel who had arrived the previous night were sleeping in the open in the sand. The CO was at his wits' end. The Army did not have a specialist designated to erect their hospitals. I don't know how they expected them to be erected. I told the hospital commander to hang in there and I would see what I could do.

After consulting with the embassy and my fleet surgeon and RADM Fellows, it was decided that we would approach the Bahraini government and see if we could get them to give us the vacant ten acres adjoining the ASU. If they would do this we would split the hospital up and put half of it beside the ASU and half of it would remain at the air base.

The Bahrainis agreed and as luck would have it we were able to find an unemployed Navy Seabee battalion overjoyed with the opportunity to establish the two sites. Within a week both halves of the hospital were functional. A real plus was that the half that was adjourning ASU had a fully functioning mess hall. Now everyone had somewhere to eat three meals a day. The CO assigned his XO to the facility at the air base and he stayed with the ASU half of the hospital. He was so appreciative that he refused to provide his daily reports to ArCent and instead gave them to me and I reported their status daily as a part of the NavCent medical report to CentCom Headquarters in Riyadh, Saudi Arabia. This continued throughout the entire war.

****

I was surprised when the ArCent Surgeon told me that he was assigning a squadron of Black Hawk MedEvac helicopters to NavCent to help with the theater MedEvac system. The problem was NavCent had two hospital ships in addition to the three 500-bed fleet hospitals. In order to utilize the MedEvac helicopters to their full extent it would require our Desert Duck helo pilots' assistance in working with the Army pilots to get them deck qualified to land on the hospital ships. We had the time as Iraq seemed to be happy with the gains they had made and were sitting still in Kuwait.

Along with the MedEvac helos we had an Air Force MedEvac radio detachment assigned to NavCent. We were really becoming a joint operation. While the MedEvac radio detachment was supposed to only use the radios for official MedEvac business, we learned quickly that it gave us an additional means of communicating with the other service headquarters and our fleet hospitals.

The MedEvac pilots were always ready to fly so we became a taxi service for most of the senior officers in the theater. We had our own dispatcher and if a request came from a Flag or general officer the dispatcher responded without further guidance. If a request came from a more junior officer the request had to be approved by either Captain Deloach or myself.

****

October 31st was to become one of the longest and worst days of my life. The USS *Iwo Jima* experienced a major boiler room break in a high pressure steam line that injured ten Sailors. I was at work when we were notified and requested assistance with medical evacuation of the injured.

Steam up to 850 degrees showered the ten men. There was little hope of saving any of them but every effort was made. One of the injured actually walked almost the length of the ship to the sick bay and was treated. He died within thirty minutes. The majority died rather quickly, but as the night went on and I listened to situation reports I had hopes that at least some would survive. It was not to be. I was notified at around 0200 on the 1st of November, the following morning, that the last of the ten had died. This was not to be the last of our naval mishaps.

On Feb 18th the USS *Tripoli* hit an Iraqi mine and sustained enough damage to take her off-line for quite a while. I do not recall them having the casualties that the *Iwo Jima* experienced.

****

As we continued to prepare for war I received word from Wanda that our youngest daughter, Jean, had married an Air Force Airman and that they were under orders to Polk Air Force Base in North Carolina. Well now it was only Wanda and I.

****

The senior medical planner on the CentCom staff was a Navy commander. He called me one day and asked if I could find him an 0-4 or an 0-5 to work with him in Riyadh, Saudi Arabia. I placed a request through medical personnel at the CNO. They identified an 0-5 and said he was to report directly to CentCom.

I called the medical planner at CentCom and he thanked me for the help. Well, it turned out to be not much help. The individual that reported was an ex-Navy Seal. When he was commissioned into the Medical Service Corps he was no longer a Navy Seal. He was in Riyadh less than a week when the commander planner called and said he was sending him to me because he was more trouble than he was worth. Turns out he wanted to be in charge and have a position rather than a job.

When he arrived in Bahrain he did not stop to see me but went directly to Captain Deloach. He informed Captain Deloach that since he was senior to me he would be taking over as the senior Medical Service Corps officer on the staff. Captain Deloach asked him to remain seated and said that he would be right back. The first I heard of any of this was when Captain Deloach came into my office and asked me to arrange transportation to the airport for this egotistical commander. He was being sent home. As it turned out I knew the guy and never was impressed with him. He was sent home and when the CNO inquired we told him what had happened. CentCom had fired him and NavCent had fired him. When CNO asked we said we did not want another replacement.

I also met with the MarCent Medical Planner, who was a Navy Nurse Corps commander. She inherited the job and did not have a clue what her responsibilities were. I spent most of my time trying to explain her responsibilities to her and directing her to the appropriate people within MarCent. Finally I told her to go back to MarCent and to send me any Marine Corps planning issues and I would help if I could. I found myself doing all of the Marine Corps medical support planning as well and doing my NavCent job. My five hours of sleep were now reduced to three or four hours per night.

As more and more Coalition forces came into the theater the issues got crazier. Of course they all wanted to know how the Medical Evacuation System was working, how did they get supplies and a ton of other issues that I did not have time to deal with.

Finally, Captain Deloach and I decided to have a Coalition medical conference and try to get everyone on the same page. We sent invitations to eleven different countries. They all responded positively.

Captain Deloach and I worked feverishly to make sure we covered almost any question that they might have. We asked the CentCom VADM to do the welcoming speech and thank them for attending. He was agreeable. Captain Deloach and I thought we were finally making some progress.

The day of the meeting, CentCom did his welcoming speech and departed. I manned the slides that addressed every issue we had thought of and Captain Deloach and I tag teamed the presentation. I had a sense that something was not right after about thirty minutes into the presentation. At lunch time we realized that only about three or four of the attendees spoke English well enough to understand and the remaining had no idea what we were trying to convey. Our use of terms we were familiar with were not necessarily terms the visiting countries' medical representatives understood.

When we reconvened after lunch Captain Deloach took the opportunity to thank all of them for their attendance and the afternoon session was cancelled. Another lesson learned.

At about this point I was informed that I had been selected for promotion to commander and RADM Fellows frocked me on the spot.

One thing really good that came out of Desert Shield/Desert Storm was that we emptied every medical warehouse in the world. The U.S. military was implementing a "just in time" supply system and had plans to eliminate all of the medical warehouses throughout the world. We did that quickly with this war.

****

I seemed to be fighting one battle after another. Two of the three fleet hospitals we had were in the fourth year of a five year renovation cycle. Most of the medical equipment was at least six to seven years old. Most of the young physicians had never even seen some of the equipment in the hospital packages much less operated it. Up-to-date items such as ventilators either were not in the hospital package or were inoperable. Items such as surgical staples were not even in the hospitals.

As I made a list of the problems and went back to the CNO medical folks I of course was directed to the one captain that had the final say in matters involving the fleet hospitals. His comments to me were that some of the items the physicians were requesting, such as surgical staples, were not part of the Table of Organization for a fleet hospital, therefore they could not have them. After a lengthy discussion on the phone and two messages to CNO, I finally found some sanity. I called the Navy Surgeon General's office and explained to a RADM what was going on. He was beside himself. He told me to send a message to BuMed and that meanwhile he would bring this up with the Surgeon General himself. Well something happened because the requested items started to arrive within the week.

****

A number of countries wanted to support the Coalition forces, but did not want to directly send combat or support troops. Japan actually sent hundreds if not thousands of vehicles, mostly four-wheel-drive SUVs, but also several twenty-passenger busses. At one point it seemed that anyone above the pay grade of chief petty officer had their own private vehicle. The Australians provided surgical teams to work on the two hospital ships.

Finally all three of the fleet hospitals were up and running and both hospital ships were in the Persian Gulf.

We discovered a serious communications problem with the hospital ships. The Geneva Convention prohibited secure communications equipment aboard them.

A second class petty officer on the staff worked out this problem by having an overlay placed over all the operational waters in which the hospital ships would be operating. A grid would be developed with random numbers, letters or words placed in each grid. Each day on the mail runs to the hospital ships we would provide a new grid with specific identification. When we wanted to move one of the hospital ships we sent them an unclassified message identifying which grid we wanted them to go to.

One of the COs of one of the ships insisted on wearing a Command at Sea badge rather than the authorized Command Ashore badge. His justification was he was on a ship and he was a CO; but in fact he was the CO of the hospital on a hospital ship, not the entire ship. The ship had a civilian master from the Military Sea Lift Command. Rear Admiral Fellows asked me several times to explain to the CO that he was not eligible to wear the Command at Sea Badge. When I broached the subject with the him he just laughed and said he did not agree. Well after repeated attempts to correct this situation I reported to RADM Fellows that the captain had refused to comply with the admiral's directions. Rear Admiral Fellows told me to contact the captain and have him report to the NavCent Chief of Staff. When the captain came to NavCent he came to see me and asked what the issue was? I told him to look at his command device and he would understand. He smiled and said well I guess we need to go see the Chief of Staff.

When we arrived at the Chief of Staff's office he directed me to have a seat and he knocked on the RADM's door and informed him that the captain was there. The Chief of Staff directed the captain to enter the RADM's office and he closed the door. Door closed or not it was not hard to hear the ass chewing that was taking place next door. The final word from RADM Fellows to the captain was that the next time he saw him if he was wearing the Command at Sea Badge he would relieve him of his command and send him home. The captain came out of RADM Fellows's office with a beet red face and without even looking at the Chief of Staff or me he walked out of the office. Needless to say he was wearing a Command Ashore Badge the next time I saw him. And once again I thought there is another senior medical department officer that I have pissed off.

TWENTY-FIVE

W ELL WE CAME TO FIGHT AND THE TIME FOR FIGHTING finally came
on the 17th of January 1991. President Bush gave General Davis
the order to remove Iraqi forces from Kuwait. It started with a massive
bombing campaign of Iraqi forces and main command-and-control
targets in Kuwait and Iraq. The highly technical, superior weapons of the
U.S. were on display for the entire world to see. The use of "smart
bombs" destroyed targets with minimal collateral damage. Saddam
Hussein's initial response was to launch his highly inaccurate SCUD
missiles into Saudi Arabia, Israel and Bahrain. He got lucky and one of
the missiles landed in an American Air Force barracks in Saudi Arabia
killing a number of Air Force personnel. His shots at Israel were an
attempt to get Israel to enter the conflict and hopefully elicit other Arab
nations to enter the war on his side. The U.S. was able to keep Israel from
retaliating. As I said, we did receive one missile in Bahrain, but all it did
was make a big hole in the ground in an unpopulated area. By February
28 the war was over and General Davis called a cease fire. On March 3
General Davis accepted the surrender of Iraqi generals.

I was in Kuwait the day after the initial assault began; the malicious
destruction of public and private property by the Iraqi occupation forces
was extensive. There was not an automobile with tires on it and
slaughtered livestock were everywhere. Every building was either shelled
or set afire.

We followed the attack into Iraq and the so-called highway of death
was just that. The horrific loss of Iraqi life and equipment defied
description. There were at least 25,000 Iraqis killed on that road. Later,
after the Iraqi equipment was collected and placed in the deserts of
Kuwait, it was estimated to be the at least four corps worth of equipment

that was captured or destroyed. A corps is composed of two or more divisions. A division routinely consists of 20,000 troops. Four corps were at least equal to 120,000 personnel and their equipment. Many of their vehicles were destroyed, but there were many that had just been abandoned.

Saddam's decision to set fire to all the oil wells was at first a great concern, but again the U.S. called upon U.S. oil industry personnel with experience in dealing with all types of oil accidents. Within days they had developed a method to extinguish the fires and cap the oil wells. Until that was accomplished the sky was so dark that at noon it appeared to be midnight. My first thoughts were what health problems were going to develop as a result of all these people breathing burning oil fumes. Again to my surprise no major health issues arose.

As soon as the cease fire was announced every U.S. military person in the theater wanted to go home. The decision was made to give priority to land-based medical personnel so that they could either resume their duties or, in the case of reserves, have them released from active duty.

That made sense but it left me with one hell of a headache. The fleet hospitals staged their equipment and got on airplanes and went home. I found that they had not gotten anyone to accept responsibility for the hospital and supporting equipment.

I captured several reserve medical personnel who were in no hurry to go home, and with RADM Fellows's blessings had them assigned to NavCent. I organized three teams to go to each of the three fleet hospitals with a manifest of equipment that was supposed to be there and had them do an inventory.

Things were quiet for a couple of days so I decided to visit the closest fleet hospital site and was almost brought to tears when the team commander reported to me the list of missing equipment and rolling stock. There was an oil tank truck, a twenty passenger bus and untold medical equipment missing. I urged them to look again closely to the equipment and four days later I found that more equipment and several four wheeled vehicles were missing. I could see that without proper security the attrition rate was going to solve any problems that I might have in shipping gear home.

I visited the other two sites and they were not doing any better. I approached RADM Fellows and explained that I did not have the manpower to protect what was remaining and that every day more equipment was disappearing.

He contacted the N-4 at the CNO's office with the problem and within two days guidance was provided that made sense. We were to approach the Saudi Arabian and Bahraini military and see if they would accept the remnants of the hospitals as a gift from the U.S. They were more than happy to accept our offer and they immediately provided the security needed to keep anymore of the equipment from disappearing.

The vice admiral, NavCent, left the theater and resumed his position as 7th Fleet in Japan.

****

We were required to put together a "lessons learned" for all of the issues, good and bad that had occurred during the war. We worked hard on the medical portion and later when I saw the finished product I was shocked. None of it made sense. I found out that since the 7th Fleet vice admiral was NavCent the lessons learned were sent through his staff for review. Well the captain that was his staff medical officer and who chose to remain onboard the ship rewrote everything that we had submitted. The final product was a totally different war than the one we had fought. He got his final say, though it probably hurt future medical planning.

TWENTY-SIX

A PERMANENT NAVCENT HEADQUARTERS WAS BEING established in Bahrain and would be a vice admiral position double hatted as Commander U.S. 5th Fleet. Before I left Bahrain for Hawaii I got news that my orders had been issued for me to be the Director for Administration at the naval hospital in Naples, Italy. Finally, as a senior Medical Service Corps officer I was being assigned to a naval hospital for the first time

There was no military housing for those of us stationed in Naples so when we reported we were given up to three weeks in a local hotel to give us time to find a home.

Right off the bat my new CO and I butted heads. The day I reported he met with me and indicated that he had been waiting for my arrival to get started on fixing a lot of broken things in the hospital command. After our initial greeting he asked me to look into an issue that was causing some problems. The issue involved a civilian worker.

I found our command civilian liaison person and got an outline of the problem and what had been done to that date. I next visited with the Civilian Personnel Office on the base and met with the civilian personnel individual that worked our command problems. After about thirty minutes of discussion I was assured that the problem would be fixed within the next forty-eight hours. He explained what had caused the problem and why it had become so confusing. Once he understood the issues he went to work fixing them. He said that he had planned to visit the hospital that afternoon to assure everyone that the problem was resolved, but since I had come to visit him there was no need for him to come to the hospital.

Every morning the CO held a "directors meeting." And during our first meeting he indicated that he also met with the directors only at 1600 each day.

The morning meeting was with all the hospital directors, i.e. Director of Nursing; Director of Medicine, Director of Ancillary Services; Director for Outlying Clinics and the Director for Administration, plus the Comptroller and our senior civilian employee. The first morning that I attended the meeting I waited to see where everyone was sitting before I took an empty seat.

When the CO came in we all came to attention and waited for him to be seated and give us permission to sit. He looked around the table and finally seemed to be satisfied with those of us present. He covered a few things that he felt we all needed to be aware of and then started around the table to give each participant an opportunity to provide input. When he got to the senior civilian he asked about the issue that he had tasked me to look into.

When the senior civilian started to give an update it was obvious that he did not have the latest information. I tried to intercede and the CO pointed his finger at me and said, "I'll tell you when to speak." I know that I turned red because I was embarrassed the first day at work with my peers. When he got to me I told him that I had nothing to offer. He smiled and said, "You had something to offer earlier, now I want to hear what you have to say." All of the other attendees were waiting to see what I would do. I thought about it for a few seconds and then told him what I had found out about the civilian employee problem and that the problem was solved. He looked at me like he could kill me. I was the last to speak and the meeting was adjourned.

I went back to my new office and thought about the meeting and decided that I could not work for a man who had no more respect for his command members than he had shown in the meeting.

I walked across that hall and went right by his secretary and walked into his office. I closed the door and that was the point at which he realized that I was in his office. I walked to the front of his desk and told him, before he had a chance to speak, that I would not work for him if he ever embarrassed me again. I told him that I would do everything within my power to support him, but if something like this happened again he needed to relieve me and call BuPers for a replacement. He was stunned. I turned and walked out of his office.

I found out that the entire hospital staff was in fear of him. He had a habit of belittling staff members in public.

He never mentioned our confrontation and neither did I. As it turned out I wound up basically running the hospital. No matter whose directorate had an issue he put me in charge of fixing the problem.

****

At one of the first 1600 meetings I was shocked when the XO, the CO and myself were the only ones present. We talked about several things and he asked what my initial impression of the command was?

I decided to be honest. I told him that I had not had much of an opportunity to go around the hospital and meet folks yet, but that my initial impression was that the hospital was dirty, the military members unkempt and that morale appeared to be low. I did not know what to expect his response to be but he surprised me. He said that he concurred and that he and I were going to change all of that.

The XO never spoke during the meeting. I found out later that this was his first hospital tour and he was a physician captain. He had spent his entire career on major fleet and force staffs. He did not know anything about hospitals and showed very little interest in learning or getting involved.

I also found out that the director for Nursing Service, a captain as well, just blew the CO off. She told me that unless something in nursing needed her attention she was leaving at 1600 every day. She said that she was a captain and she didn't have to put up with his bull. I noticed that she was always respectful to the CO, but she pretty much did as she pleased. The other directors also failed to come to the 1600 meeting, but this did not seem to bother the CO.

It was becoming clear why I had so much on my plate. The XO couldn't or wouldn't do anything, so I inherited his responsibilities.

I eventually noticed an entirely different attitude coming toward me from the CO. He grew to know that he could trust me and depend on me. However, he was still an ass. He told me that he expected to see the junior officers that worked for me to make an appearance in the hospital every weekend day. He would actually come by the hospital to see whose cars he could recognize in the parking lot on the weekends. I found out that a lot of the junior officers just parked their cars in the hospital lot and got a friend to give them a ride home. He suspected this may be happening and suggested that I go to each of their offices after they departed on Fridays and place a hair in their door and then close it. If I got there early enough on Mondays I could determine who had been in and who had not by the existence or lack of hair. I thought this guy is nuts.

I soon realized that my new CO was not only an ass, he was an intelligent ass. He knew his hospital administration inside out. I learned more working for him than I would have ever learned working for a "nice" guy.

****

My wife got a job working in the hospital but she was working for the comptroller who did not work for me, so there was no conflict of interest.

This tour of duty was a real learning experience. I found that if senior Medical Department officers did not want to do something it was difficult to force them to comply. I also learned that rank did not matter as much as opportunity and ability. I found myself in a situation were no senior officer in the command did what they were assigned to do; only what they wanted to do. This situation placed more responsibility on my plate than should have been placed there as a commander. Because of the CO's personality I found almost everyone was coming to me for action or answers. It appeared to the command that I was the only officer that the CO would listen to. And, to some extent that was probably true.

Unfortunately my work day was from 0600 until 2000, at least, and sometime even later. Wanda was stuck waiting for me every day. We found a little mom-and-pop restaurant that we loved and ate dinner there almost every night on the way home.

There are many stories that I could share about this tour, but I will limit it to just some of the real highlights.

I was two junior officers short of my requirement and I called the MSC assignment officer and asked him when I could expect them. Of course he had a dozen reasons for not having filled the billets. We struck a deal. He would continue to try to find someone to fill my empty billets but in the meantime he would send me three newly commissioned officers. Good to his word I had three new ensigns report aboard within the next two weeks. I threw them into the fire as department heads and talked to the senior enlisted member in each department and explained that their job was to "respectfully" teach the ensigns their jobs. It worked out fairly well. All three were go-getters and anxious to learn.

Also good to his word within a month I had an LTJG on her second tour report aboard and a full LT reported a day or two later. This was about the time that all the Army and Air Force bases in Europe were being disestablished or drawn down significantly.

I had already called a couple of the Army and Air Force medical facilities about what they were going to do with their excess equipment. They said that we could have anything they had that we could use.

To this day I am not sure if my next move was a smart move or a dumb one. I called the new LT into my office and told him to go to every directorate and get a wish list of equipment that they would like to have. I told him to emphasize to them that the sky was the limit. I told him I wanted the list within one week.

The following week to the day he returned to my office with several volumes of "want and must have" lists. He was stunned when I gave him his next order. Go to every military hospital in Europe that is being closed or downsized and obtain everything that you can that is on that list. I had his Temporary Additional Duty Orders (TAD) prepared with an open end return date. I gave him a government credit card and provided him a rental car and said goodbye. I did tell him that he was to account for everything he put on that charge card.

He was gone about ten days and I had not heard from him. One morning the quarterdeck petty officer called my office and said that I needed to come to the front of the hospital. When I arrived he just pointed out the front door. There was an eighteen-wheeler truck out front. I went out to see what was going on and was told that the truck was full of medical supplies and where did I want them delivered?

The comptroller wanted to play games with me in that he would not share any financial information with me. He was a LT and I was a commander. I went to the CO and discussed the truck out front and told him I needed the money to rent a warehouse but could not get any information out of the Comptroller. The CO told me to go to the contracting officer on the main base and get him to find us a warehouse. The CO said that he would take care of the Comptroller. I don't know where the money came from but we contacted for a 9,000 square foot warehouse in downtown Naples. I assigned a chief petty officer and four enlisted to work at the warehouse. Within the next two weeks the warehouse was full. I could not find my LT to stop him. Finally he called me from somewhere in Spain and said that he had two more trucks on the way and that he was headed for home. Thank God!

To my surprise one of the things he was able to get was a trailer with a CT scanner in it. Our ability to diagnose issues went up significantly. He had met every director's need and then some. Once we sorted out what we needed I informed BuMed that I had excess equipment and that any hospital willing to pay the freight could have it. I provided a list of the items and within two months we closed our warehouse.

****

The CO was a marathon runner and signed up for the Rome Marathon. The weekend he was gone all hell broke loose. Of course the XO was nowhere to be found. The duty officer at the hospital called me on my portable phone and told me that there had been an auto accident involving a family member of the four-star admiral's staff. The admiral was double hatted as Commander and Chief Naval Forces Europe and Commander NATO Forces Southern Europe. He maintained his office in Naples for NATO versus London where Naval Forces Europe Headquarters were located.

By the time I arrived at the hospital and had unraveled what was going on things appeared to be moving in the right direction. The death was the mother of the wife of the admiral's aide. We had our senior Italian civilian working on the case with the Italian authorities. The aide had been afforded an office where he could make phone calls with a degree of privacy. I was still getting information from the duty officer when the aide, who was standing there listening in, was told by the sailor at the front desk that he had a phone call and the sailor said he would patch it through to the office the aide had been using. The aide said, "No problem, I can take it here."

He was on the phone at the front desk when Admiral Roland came through the front door. When he saw his aide on the phone in the foyer he went nuts. He turned to the duty officer and started to yell at him for his insensitivity. I explained to the admiral that I was the senior hospital member present and that I would do everything possible to assist the aide and his family. Thank God he shut up long enough for his aide to explain that we had given him a private office and that it was his choice to take the current call at the front desk.

The admiral requested that he be directed to the CO's office because he needed to make some phone calls. When we got there the main door was locked and we could not find a key. Thankfully the duty officer found a key to a door that opened from the hallway into the CO's office. When the admiral sat down at the CO's desk he asked me which of the phone lines on that multi-line phone was an autovon (a military dedicated phone line) line. I had never been behind the CO's desk and did not have a clue. This sent him into another fit of rage. He figured it out and made his phone call to whomever.

When he arrived back in the emergency room area the aide and my senior Italian civilian employee, who had been working at the hospital for over forty years, were discussing the issue of obtaining his mother-in-law's body. The senior Italian was assuring the aide that it would be difficult on the weekend, but promised that he could get the body released to us first thing tomorrow morning. When the admiral arrived his first question was, "What are we doing about getting the body released to the hospital?" When I explained to him that we were just discussing that issue and we would be able to gain custody of the body first thing tomorrow morning, he went off again. Raising his voice he said, "Bull! I want that body today and with no more delays." The aide finally spoke up and told the admiral that he had talked to his wife and she was comfortable with tomorrow morning. The admiral was not satisfied, but it did calm him down.

The remainder of the day was spent making arrangements to transport the body to the U.S. The admiral authorized military transport to the States.

The admiral was not happy with the fact that the C.O and the X.O. could not be located. This was not to be the last run-in between the admiral and the hospital.

****

The next issue was ships complaining about getting their crew members back after they were sent to the hospital for treatment. This was an issue that I had brought up with the CO of Naval Support Activity. We were treating the patients and as soon as their treatment allowed we transferred them to the transient facility at the Naval Support Activity. The bottleneck was there. The OIC of the transient facility was not making the ships, or in many cases the individual's, assignment personnel aware that the patient care was complete and that it was requested that arrangements be made to either return the members to their command or re-assign them to another unit.

The admiral's Chief of Staff called one afternoon and told the CO that the admiral wanted the CO. and his person responsible for patient administration to be in his office at 0900 the following day. The CO informed me that he and I were going to be going to see the admiral the next morning.

We were at the admiral's office at 0845 the following morning and since it was a NATO headquarters, members of several countries were present for the morning meeting.

We all filed into the large conference room and the NATO officers took their places at the huge conference table. The Chief of Staff seated the CO and me in chairs along the wall. The NATO officers seemed to be curious about us being there but said nothing.

The admiral conducted his morning meeting with the NATO officers and when it was concluded he asked my CO if I was the person responsible for patient administration. The CO responded in the affirmative. The admiral asked his aide who was seated to his immediate left to please swap seats with me.

I joined the group at the table.

The admiral began to explain about the fleet complaints regarding their problems getting personnel returned to them after their treatment was completed. The admiral went to great lengths to explain that he was an expert in transient personnel movement business and that he had actually created an organization in New Orleans to track and ensure that transients worldwide were being properly processed and returned to a "for duty status." He indicated that when he was the N-3 at the Bureau of Naval Personnel, he had assigned a group of specialists in the Navy personnel field to a new unit called the Navy Transient Monitoring Unit (TMU). He suggested that I contact this group and request they come to Naples to conduct an audit of the patient processing procedures.

I think my next comment almost caused him to faint. I told him that I had in fact been in touch with the TMU, explaining that the problems we were having were with the Naval Support Activity's Transient Personnel Unit. I also told him that I was quite familiar with the unit as I had served a tour as the OIC of TMU. He looked at me as if I were crazy. He asked when I was the OIC and who did I relieve. I told him and he knew the officer I had relieved quite well.

He asked what was a Medical Service Corps officer doing being assigned to the TMU? I told him that the TMU had been quite effective with all Navy transient problems except patient administration. I explained that I had served in military personnel billets several times, including helping to set up the new Navy base oriented personnel offices. While I was the OIC of TMU we completely rewrote the patient processing portion of the Navy's *Enlisted Transfer Personnel Manual.* I also mentioned that the TMU received a letter or appreciation from the secretary of the Navy for our efforts during my tour. Though he was stunned he smiled and said, "I guess I don't need to tell you how to manage patient transient personnel." He thanked me for coming and dismissed me and the CO.

I think the admiral started to look at me a little differently after that meeting, but it did not get him off of the hospital's case.

****

Another continuing issue was his daughter. She had been married to a naval officer and they had produced a child. Later they divorced. The daughter was living with her father, Admiral Roland, in Naples and on several occasions I received a call from her mother because the child was not getting what she considered timely appointments when she experienced a problem. Occasionally, the daughter would present herself for treatment. She was not eligible for care and because she could not produce a dependent's identification card she was turned away. Well the admiral knew that this was proper, but that did not stop him from calling me directly and asking if there were some way we could see his daughter because he did not want to send her to the Italian medical facilities. I thought for a second and asked him to have her come to see me anytime she had a problem and I would see that she was taken care of. The first time she came she had her mother with her and it was obvious that they were expecting problems. I took her to the family practice clinic and told the clinic director that the CO had authorized her's as a humanitarian case, since the Italian medical facilities did not offer English speaking caregivers, which made it difficult for Americans to receive adequate care. There were no further problems with her, but there were more problems to come from the admiral.

****

One Monday morning I received a call from the emergency room requesting that I come down. When I got there, there were two elderly ladies sitting in the waiting room. One was obviously in pain.

The emergency room director said that the lady in pain had fallen and busted her elbow in Rome while vacationing. That she had gone to the U.S. Embassy and they directed her to our hospital as we were the closest U.S. medical facility.

I asked the doctor what was the issue. He said that he had examined her and thought we should do x-rays to determine the extent of the injury. I told him no problem, this was an emergency and a humanitarian requirement.

After the x-rays the doctor and an orthopedic surgeon determined that the injury was sufficiently serious that she should have surgery, and they did not recommend waiting for her to get back to the States.

We approached the injured lady and explained what the doctors had determined and asked if she was willing to sign a release and have the surgery here in our hospital. She did not hesitate to agree.

She was taken to the surgery prep area and I asked the other lady, who happened to be her twin sister, if there was anything I could do for her while the surgery was being performed. She asked if there was any way she could make a phone call to the States. I said certainly and took her to my office and let her use my phone. I told her that I would be across the hall when she finished and that I would then take her to the hospital surgery waiting area.

About forty-five minutes later I received a call from the quarter deck indicating that the admiral had just come through the front entrance and was on his way to mine or the CO's office.

I was waiting for him when he stepped off the elevator. He was obviously upset. He stood with his hands on his hips and literally yelled at me, "When are you idiots going to learn that I need to be informed when something like this occurs?" I had no idea what his issue was and told him so. He asked, "Do you know who you people are operating on at this minute?" I did not know who she was but I knew it could only be the little old lady with the busted elbow. I said, "Admiral, I assume you are referring to the elderly lady who presented with a busted elbow." He informed me that the "little old lady" was the mother of a U.S. senator. I thought, "Oh crap." I tried to explain that she had never indicated that she had political connections and we had no reason to ask. I guess the sister's phone call was to the senator and he called the Pentagon and they in turn called the admiral. My answer was not satisfactory to him but at least I think he was beginning to give us the benefit of the doubt. I took him to the CO's office and explained to the CO what was going on. I left them to have what I am sure was a not so friendly chat.

****

We had another admiral in the area who was just the opposite of the four-star. This admiral was a newly promoted RADM, lower half, and he was the senior Navy commander in the Naples area. We had some social function that had an open bar at the NATO Club and we invited RADM Robinson.

My first actual meeting with him was at a social. As he came in I was there to greet him and take him around to meet and greet other members of our staff. He asked me if the bar was an open bar. I said, "Yes, Sir, this is a pay-as-you-go affair. He looked at me sheepishly and asked if I by chance had 10,000 Italian lire because he did not being any money with him. I did not hesitate and as we walked to the bar I slipped him the 10,000 and bought him and I a drink. He smiled and said he would get the next one.

When I introduced him to my wife she had to take that opportunity to tell him that we were brand new grandparents. Our first grandson, Tim, had just been born. He congratulated us. I did not want him to feel that he was stuck with me all night so when I introduced him to the XO and his wife I took that opportunity to excuse myself and told him that if he needed anything that I would be in the area until the party was over.

The following Monday morning RADM Robinson's aide knocked on my door and came in and handed me an envelope. He said it was from RADM Robinson. Of course the envelope contained a 10,000 lire note.

We had two or three other social events that RADM Robinson was invited to and at each one he smiled and said, "Did you bring my 10,000 lire?" I smiled back and discreetly gave him the money. Without fail his aide was in my office the next business day with an envelope from RADM Robinson. I could tell the aide wanted to ask what was going on, but discretion was the better part of valor.

I was not surprised when I heard that RADM Robinson had been selected for his second star and was transferring to a fleet command. I was glad that I was on the downward side of my tour in Italy, because I would certainly miss RADM Robinson.

****

As we should have expected, the day came when my CO came into my office and said that he had just received a phone call from the admiral's office saying that the admiral wanted to see him at 1400 this afternoon. I asked if he knew what the issue was. He shook his head no and said, "I think I am about to be relieved of my command." I was shocked. He asked me to wait around until he returned.

When he returned he was a beaten man. I knew the news was not going to be good. He told me to prepare for a change of command ceremony for the 30th of the next month. I said, "Did he give you any other options?" He said yes: it was retire or be relieved.

The new CO knew nothing about running a hospital but he was a very nice individual and the morale started to improved immediately.

Shortly after the new CO arrived we also got a new XO. He was also a nice enough guy but I could see he was not going to sit on his behind and let me run the hospital. It was ok with me because I only had about three months left on my tour and my relief had already been identified.

To my surprise, about three days after the XO arrived I was called by the NATO Chief of Staff to the senior U.S. RADM, who informed me that I was being transferred to him in a temporary duty status to help develop the medical portion of an operational plan to relieve the United Nations (UN) personnel currently in Bosnia/Herzegovina and Serbia. It was believed that the U.N. may have to implement military action to get their forces out of the conflict. I informed my CO and he made a couple of calls and told me there was nothing he could do. The good news was that I had two or three junior officers who could administratively help out him and the XO.

****

I finished my tour in Naples by working for NATO up until the last two weeks before my departure.

I was ready to go, but Wanda and I had developed some strong attachments to many of the Neapolitans and a love for the country. The best part of leaving was that I was going to the job that I had always wanted. I was going to be the assignment officer (detailer) for the administrative Medical Service Corps officers in the Navy.

TWENTY-SEVEN

Wanda AND I ARRIVED IN WASHINGTON, D.C. AND had little problem finding a nice Town House in the Alexandria area of Virginia. We had lots of options with an empty nest, but did not want to live in the Arlington area, which would be near to where I worked, but more of a commute problem for Wanda who had already secured a job in the Manpower Office for the Naval Hospital, Bethesda, Maryland. This was a great job for her because she was able to retain the GS-12 rating that she had earned during our Naples tour.

During this tour the Navy was trying to reduce expenses and developed an early retirement program for civilian employees who met certain criteria. Wanda read the criteria and determined that she was eligible for retirement. With my blessings she submitted her application and it was approved. She was retiring at a reduced retirement rate, but never again would she be looking for a job when I transferred, and never again would she have to take a lower grade job just to have a job. Life for me after she retired was so much better and she took over most of our household chores herself. No longer would I have to empty our cat Haole's litter box.

****

When I reported in to the Bureau of Naval Personnel I was happy to know that my boss was none other than Captain Bruce Russel, who had worked wonders to get me to Hawaii after my assignment to the Armed Forces Staff College. Bruce and I became lifelong friends and great fishing buddies. Bruce was the captain department head responsible for the assignment of all Medical Department officers, physicians, nurses, and allied scientists (pharmacy, physical therapy, etc.).

I also found out that one of my favorite admirals, Admiral Robinson, was now a vice admiral and the Chief of Naval Personnel. We were so far removed from one another I doubted that we would ever meet during my tour.

Bruce informed me that he had been successful in obtaining a LCDR Billet that I could use to bring in an assistant detailer. This had always been a one man shop, but I could see real advantages to having a junior MSC officer to assist me. At the time of my arrival Bruce had already pulled one of the officers from his Placement Division to help the captain that I was relieving. So I had an assistant, but I had to find a relief for her as her projected rotation date (PRD) was coming up in about six months.

My first thought was who would fill this position. It did not take me long to come up with an answer—Edward, my LT who did all of the medical shopping when the Army and Air Force hospitals were being closed. When I left Naples he was the director for the Hospital's branch clinics. There were six branch clinics in two different countries. He was selected for LCDR but he was still very junior for the director's job. I called him that day and offered him the job. Of course he was curious about what he would be doing. I told him that he would be assigning the bulk of the administrative Medical Service Corps officers. He would be responsible for assignment of all ensigns, LTJGs and LTs. He asked if he could talk it over with his wife and call me right back. His concern was he had twin boys in high school and was concerned about bringing them to the D. C. area.

Edward called back about three hours later and accepted the job. I wrote his orders within the next fifteen minutes. He would not be onboard for at least three more months.

After Edward arrived and we worked out the details of his assignment he jumped right into the job of assigning his junior officers. I made it clear to him that any contentious assignments would be referred to me. In our almost three years of working together I can only recall two or three situation where I had to get involved and I supported his decisions every time, because he was making the right decision.

While this was a strenuous assignment for both of us we broke a lot of new ground. The entire Medical Assignment Department only had one computer. There was an internal computer system that BuPers had established but it was cumbersome and totally unreliable. I had to meet with the Chief of the Medical Service Corps, a RADM lower-half, later on a RADM upper-half. The purpose of these meetings was to keep him informed on any issues that may be reflected back to him as the senior Medical Service Corps officer in the Navy. Frequently if someone did not like an assignment they received they would try to end run the detailer and go to the Chief of the Corps to try and exert influence on the assignment. While technically I did not work for the Chief of the Medical Service Corps, he was under the Chief of BuMed and I was under the Chief of Naval Personnel, he and I had a vested issue in working together.

Fortunately, BuMed was getting all new computers and I asked if it were possible for the BuPers medical detailers to receive the computers that BuMed was getting rid of. He said that if I could get BuPers's permission that he would see that we got the computers.

Well we got the computers. That did not make everyone happy because along with the computers came the ability for our constituents to send us email, which added to the workload because we had to answer them.

One of the first issues I brought to the Chief of the Corps was the fact that I had found a number of senior MSCs who were homesteading in the D.C. area and in some of the other major naval areas around the country. Some were not even in valid billets. I told him it was my intention to move these senior officers or force them into retirement. He looked at me, laughed and said, "Good luck."

I picked my first candidate to see if I could be successful. He was a captain who was at the Naval Hospital Bethesda and was not assigned to a valid billet. I did not call him and discuss anything with him; I just wrote him a set of orders to the 4th Marine Division, a reserve Marine division, in New Orleans. There was a vacant captain's billet at the 4th Marine Division Headquarters.

He received his orders two days later and called me to see what I was thinking. I explained the facts to him about him not being in a valid billet and that he was on his fourth tour of duty in the D.C. area.

Well it did not take long before he had the CO at Bethesda calling me requesting that I rethink this decision. I explained to the RADM commanding officer that this was not negotiable. He asked what the captain's options were. I said, "Execute his orders or have retirement papers on my desk within seventy-two hours."

The next day the captain was standing at my desk when I came to work. He had a request for retirement in his hands but requested an opportunity to speak with Captain Bruce Russel, my boss. I took him to Bruce's office and Bruce asked me to stay. The captain asked that his orders to the 4th Marine Division be rescinded. Bruce asked me what was going on and I explained to him the issue and informed him that the captain's CO had even called me about the possibility of rescinding the orders. Bruce looked at the captain and said, "Captain, I think Commander Sullivan has given you two options so you need to consider which you are going to accept." Dejectedly the captain handed Bruce his request for retirement. I had won my first round.

My next visit with the Chief of the Medical Service Corps was interesting. He smiled and said, "I did not think you would get him out of Bethesda." He informed me that the RADM at Bethesda had called him about the assignment and that he had informed the RADM that assignment of Medical Service Corps officers was a BuPers responsibility and he had no control over it. He said he suggested that the RADM contact the Chief of Naval Personnel, a vice admiral if he wanted to pursue this issue. The RADM opted not to do so.

With that success under my belt I went after the next captain who had been in the D.C. area for almost fifteen years. He had been extended in his current billet three times for a year each. I took the same approach with him as I had with the first captain. But the results were quite different. I was finding that the 4th Marine Division assignment was not one that captains were lusting after. It was the perfect billet to get actions when dealing with senior captains.

This captain had a little more political influence than the previous one and he worked for a RADM upper-half who did call the Chief of Naval Personnel complaining about the assignment. At some point after the phone call Bruce came over and said that his boss, another captain, but a line captain, had just informed him that he, Bruce and I had an appointment with the Chief of Naval Personnel at 1400 that afternoon.

That gave me about two hours to brief Bruce and his boss about what was going on. In my effort to ensure that I had all my ducks in a row I had completely forgotten that we were going to see Vice Admiral Robinson.

When we arrived in the Chief of Naval Personnel's office his Chief of Staff, a captain, said it would be a few minutes before the Chief could see us. He offered coffee which no one desired.

A few minutes later the Chief of Staff said that we should follow him into the admiral's office. When we came through the door I was the junior officer so I was last in the procession. Vice Admiral Robinson shook hands with Bruce's boss, and then while shaking hands with Bruce he noticed me. A big smile came across his face and he asked me if I happen to have 10,000 lire handy. I could see the confusion on Bruce's boss's face as well as on Bruce's. Admiral Robinson asked me how Tim was doing. I could not believe he even remembered that I had a grandson, much less his name. He then said, "I did not know that you worked for me, why didn't come down before now"? He knew that I would not have considered paying him a social visit, but the comment was nice.

Bottom line, after hearing what I was doing, and that I had the support of the Chief of the Medical Service Corps, he said for us to go back to work he would take care of the issue. As we departed he followed us to the door and grabbed my shoulder and gave me an almost affectionate hug.

I did not realize that I had upset Bruce's boss. As soon as we were out of hearing range of the admiral's office he lit into me. He said that I had embarrassed him by not telling him that I knew the admiral. I tried to explain that I had no idea that the admiral would even remember me, that I had not worked for him directly. He asked what the 10,000 lire comment all about. I told him that once at a social function, with an open bar, in Naples, Italy, the admiral showed up at the function with no Italian money and I loaned him 10,000 lire. I was not about to tell him that this had been a repeated affair. This was not to be the last time I got under the skin of Bruce's boss.

I had won round two. It was time to get serious.

****

The word was out that this new detailer was cleaning out homesteaders in the D. C. area. I only had to cut two more sets of orders to the 4th Marine Division before I had the entire deadwood captains retired.

However, I finally found a taker to the 4th Marine Division when I cut orders to a captain in San Diego. The CO of the naval hospital, a RADM, had his Director for Administration call me and ask if I could get this captain out of San Diego. It appears he had been the previous Director for Administration and was occupying assigned quarters even though he was no longer assigned to the naval hospital.

When I hit this captain with orders to the 4th Marine Division he called in a panic. He said that he had twin sons that would be entering their junior year in high school and he could not take them to New Orleans. I gave him the choice, execute the orders or send me a retirement request. He executed his orders to New Orleans and went unaccompanied. His wife and sons were forced to move out of the assigned quarters, but they stayed in San Diego.

Thank goodness I had pretty much cleaned up the captain homesteaders because I had lost my biggest threat, the 4th Marine Division.

****

I was a very senior commander so when the captains' promotion list came out and I was selected for captain I was the third one on the promotion list. The first two were selected from the previously passed over list which made them senior to me.

When my promotion day was arriving I asked my good friend, Fran, the previous Chief of Nursing Service in Naples, if she would promote me. I told her that I wanted to do the promotion in my hometown of Columbia. She was excited. I got all of the promotion papers prepared and Wanda and I took a week of leave and met Captain Fran and her husband, Bill, in Columbia. We obtained DIV quarters in a cabin by a lake at Fort Jackson.

When we returned and I was wearing my captain's eagles, Bruce's boss went off like a loose cannon. He stood in my face and asked who authorized me to have my promotion done by someone other than him. I said, "I did not know that you wanted to do my promotion. I certainly did not do this to upset you; I just wanted my friend to do the promotion." I could tell he was upset, but he just turned and walked away.

****

There were a couple of assignments that would cause me problems. I knew when I made them that there would be questions or problems, but I thought they were acceptable assignments.

The first was a commander who was also a D.C. homesteader, but his current tour was up. He wanted another assignment to the D.C. area but I had an urgent need for an OIC at the Naval Hospital Naples' branch clinic at La Maddalena, Sardinia. When I suggested this to the commander he said, "You have got to be kidding me." I said, "No it is a must fill for me and you have no management assignments in your past, and this is needed to keep you competitive for captain." He was really upset to have to leave the D.C. area, but he had little choice once he had his orders in hand.

Well I should have known that he would try to get back to D.C. one way or another. When he got to La Maddalena he became a big problem for his staff and they complained to the CO in Naples. After about two months the CO relieved him and brought him back to Naples awaiting orders. I told the CO that I would write him orders but he was not going to be happy with those orders either. The orders were to a medical training command in San Diego.

When his orders arrived he came through D.C. on his way to San Diego and immediately went to see the Navy Inspector General (IG).

I was somewhat surprised to see a captain waiting in my cubicle when I came back from lunch. I asked if I could assist him with something and he said he was from the Navy IG's office and he was investigating a complaint that had been filed against me. I asked who filed the complaint and what the issue was. Well I was not surprised to find out it was my favorite commander from La Maddalena. I inquired as to what was the complaint. The captain said, "Racial discrimination." I said, "Oh? What race does he claim to be?" The captain said, "American Indian." I did not say anything I just pulled up my record on the BuPers computer and pointed to my race.

The captain looked and saw that my race was American Indian. He shook his head and said it was now the easiest complaint he had ever worked. He smiled and said, "Case closed, and thank you for your time."

The other problem assignment was a fair-haired female commander who worked for the Deputy Chief of BuMed. She had been tied to his coattails for several years and as he advanced he brought her along with him. The problem was she was overweight and had been sent through the weight control program twice and still gained her weight back after the program.

She came to me and asked if I would consider assigning her to the naval hospital in Pensacola, Florida as the Director for Administration. She was also married to an LCDR MSC and she pointed out that the Director for Administration position at the naval dental clinic in Pensacola was also available and that her husband was willing to take that assignment if she could go to the hospital. I told her that I did not know if I could even assign her anywhere with her weight problem, but that I'd do some research.

I went to see the department in BuPers that ran the Navy's Weight Control Program. I explained what I was considering and asked them if that was possible. They showed me an article in their manual that addressed this issue and basically I could make this assignment, but only if the CO was aware of her problem and he was willing to accept her.

Most all of the senior officers in the Medical Service Corps knew each other so I knew the CO at Pensacola very well, and he not only knew me but he knew this overweight commander. I gave him a call and put the issue to him. He was quiet for a few minutes and then asked if he could think about it and call me back.

The next day he called me back and said he would accept her. I was somewhat surprised but informed her that I was writing her and her husband's orders to Pensacola. I thought that was the end of it but it was not. Later in my next tour this assignment came back to haunt me.

There were very few issues with most of my assignments and most worked out well for the individual and the Navy. My tour was normally two years, but I was asked to stay a little longer because BuPers was moving to Millington, Tennessee and they did not want me to bring someone in to D.C. for six months and then move them to Millington.

****

Meanwhile, I was looking for my next assignment. There was a vacant captain's billet in Key West, Florida, that was coming available and matched up with my Projected Rotation Date (PRD). Wanda and I discussed this billet. It was the OIC of the branch medical clinic. As the OIC I would be subordinate to the CO of the naval hospital in Jacksonville, Florida. We decided that while it would be fun to live in Key West for a couple of years we did not want to make that a retirement home area. I assigned another newly promoted captain to that billet.

I had been told that I was being considered for the XO billet at Naval Hospital Corpus Christi, Texas. The CO was a single nurse corps officer whom I knew and admired. However, two things entered into that decision. First, the CO was very soft spoken and I do not ever recall having a conversation with her where I could hear her well enough to feel comfortable. Next, we wanted to make this next assignment our final assignment and we wanted to retire in Florida. Another big choice was made when I informed Bruce that I did not want to be considered for an executive officer position. He was somewhat taken aback but said he would inform the powers to be to take me off of the list of potential XOs.

I had my eye on a billet that did not quite match up with my PRD, but the incumbent had been in the billet long enough that I would not have to get permission from Bruce or his boss to move him a little early. The billet was as the Medical War Planner at U. S. Central Command in Tampa, Florida. The incumbent was none other than my assistant from Desert Storm, Captain Select Phillip Hayes. I had the CO's billet at 3rd Medical Battalion with the 3rd Marine Division in Okinawa available and I thought that Phillip would like to have that opportunity.

I called Phillip and discussed this opportunity with him and he was not hesitant to say yes. He asked me who I had in mind to replace him. I told him that I was thinking about assigning myself to the billet. He said that I would love the assignment and asked when this was to occur. I said that he would be moving in about three months.

My tour came to an end and Wanda and I headed to Tampa, me with my fifth Meritorious Service Medal.

We had a tough time finding the right retirement home but finally found the perfect one in a gated community with a freshwater canal behind our house. The community was on a freshwater system but, had two boatlifts that were available to lift our boats over into the saltwater canal that led to Tampa Bay and the Gulf of Mexico.

TWENTY-EIGHT

I REPORTED INTO U.S. CENTRAL COMMAND AND WAS surprised that I was the only Sailor on the medical staff of the CentCom Surgeon. There were six Army medical personnel, including the Deputy Surgeon, and two Air Force personnel including the surgeon.

The Command Surgeon was an Air Force colonel named Hall who would eventually be the Surgeon General of the Air Force.

There was no major operations plan being worked at the moment and only a couple of conceptual plans being reviewed.

The Command Surgeon had an Army lieutenant colonel operations officer, but he was not a go-getter. The Surgeon decided to use me as an additional operations officer. I knew that I could keep the plans up-to-date and still work the operational officer billet. He suggested that I make an orientation trip to the Middle East and based upon my contacts in the various countries determine what we could do to enhance our medical status in those countries.

I had to contact the U.S. embassies in each of the countries that I was planning to visit. Of course they insisted on sending an embassy official with me on each trip. What I was looking for was warehouse space to preposition Army and Navy field and fleet hospitals.

I went to Bahrain first and met with the minister of health. We discussed a number of issues, but Bahrain seemed to have a good working relationship with the Naval Support Activity and the 5th Fleet staff. And, we already had an Army field hospital prepositioned in Bahrain, so decided not to pursue additional space in Bahrain. I assured the minister of health that we were available if he needed anything.

Next I went to Kuwait. The minister of health was also the CEO of the only military hospital in Bahrain. Dr. Mohamsa immediately requested that we develop a closer working relationship with his military hospital. We still had a significant military presence in Kuwait. And when any of our military members needed care beyond the capabilities of our small medical facilities they were brought to the Kuwaiti military hospital for care.

He asked if it were possible for us to help him bring his hospital up to U. S. standards as required by the Joint Commission on the Accreditation of Health Care Organizations (JCAHO). I told him that I would see what I could do to put together a team to come back and take a look at his hospital.

He also took advantage of the fact that his hospital was treating U.S. personnel to ask if it was feasible to assign some U.S. surgical personnel to his hospital. Again I told him I would have to go back and discuss these issues with my CinC Surgeon. I left with a commitment for Kuwait to provide warehouse space for an Army field hospital. The location would be in close proximity to the Kuwaiti military hospital.

I then went to Qatar and met with their minister of health. When I broached the subject of pre-positioning an Army field hospital or a Navy fleet hospital the minister was all for assisting us with providing warehouse space to preposition two such hospitals. I thanked him and assured him that I would be back in touch with him within the next month or so.

I felt that I need to go home and discuss these issues with the CinC Surgeon. When I briefed him on my trip it was apparent that he was pleased with my efforts. He immediately briefed the CinC. He got permission from the CinC for us to pursue all of these initiatives.

With the Surgeon's assistance we first put together a team of experts in all of the areas of hospital administration and operations from primarily the Army and Air Force. I had a team of eighteen physicians, nurses, administrators, logistics personnel and security personnel that deployed with me to Kuwait to try and provide a simulated JCAHO survey to try and determine what would be needed to bring the hospital up to U.S. standards.

It became apparent early on that this was going to present some real problems and would require some real diplomacy on my part to keep from offending the Kuwaitis. Their culture and ours were significantly different.

One of the first issues to come up was the doctor's bathroom in the emergency room area. There was no soap, paper towels or toilet paper in the bathroom. There was a community hand towel that everyone used. Since they used a bidet and their left hand to clean themselves after using the toilet they did not need toilet paper. God knows what they thought about washing their hands with no soap and drying them again on the community towel.

I asked for a meeting with Dr. Mohamsa and during the course of the meeting I mentioned the cultural differences and that some things that the Kuwaiti doctors would have to adjust to some required changes if he were to meet JCAHO standards. I explained the issue with the emergency room doctor's bathroom and he did not seem to be offended at all. He said that he would see that the issue was corrected within the next day or so. I began to understand that Dr. Mohamsa had experience with Western medical facilities and he realized that his hospital would have to make some major changes to accomplish what he wanted done. He had obviously briefed his staff in the hospital because every one of them was very cooperative and more than willing to assist in our efforts.

Good to his word the next day there were paper towel dispensers, soap dishes and hand soap, along with toilet paper available in the emergency room physician's bathroom.

Meanwhile Colonel Hall was working with the Army, Navy, and Air Force Components to see if keeping a U.S. surgical team in the Kuwaiti hospital on a rotating basis was feasible and would they support the effort by providing the necessary personnel. All of the components were supportive and it was decided that each would take a three month rotation in the Kuwaiti military hospital. The CinC Surgeon contacted me and I was able to share with Dr. Mohamsa that his desire to have a permanent U.S. surgical team in his hospital was approved and with his permission we were prepared to send the first team the first of the following month. He was so excited he called someone in his hierarchy and with jubilation shared this information with him.

With the results of our survey in hand I briefed Dr. Mohamsa and told him that I would take it back home and polish it up and provide him a written report that would assist him in making changes to his hospital. He was very gracious and requested that I come back often.

The first U.S. surgical team had been onboard less than a week when there were five U.S. military personnel involved in a serious automobile accident and they were brought to the Kuwaiti military hospital for care. They were very happy to see that they were going to be treated by U.S. doctors. The surgical teams were provided living space in the one of the hospital's wards that was not in use. They took all their meals in the hospital dining facility. This rotation between the services continued up until they were removed just prior to the second Gulf War.

****

The CinC Surgeon was one of the best bosses I had ever had. He gave me general directions and gave me my lead to do the job however I desired.

I eventually got back to my primary job of war planning when one of our major operations plans was up for review. However, I had so much going on in the Middle East that it was hard to stay in Tampa. I was burning the candle at both ends and it seemed that between working late nights on the operation plan and flying back and forth to the Middle East I physically was starting to feel the effects. Because there were from five to seven time zone differences between Tampa and the Middle Eastern countries I was living on sleeping pills. It always seemed that I arrived in the middle of the night and had either an early morning or mid-morning meeting to attend. Frequently when I arrived at home there were tickets on my desk for me to return to a different country in the Middle East.

About this time an issue from my tour as the MSC detailer came back to haunt me. One morning the CinC's IG, a Navy captain, came into my cubicle and said that the Navy's IG was in his office and was requesting that he have an opportunity to speak with me. I questioned the reason for the meeting and the CinC's IG indicated that he had no idea. I said that I would meet with him. He was in one of the conference rooms and when

I arrived I saw the configuration of the meeting area and understood that he had established himself and another two civilians at a table on the elevated platform in the conference room and had a chair for me below the elevated area. He was establishing his position of authority. He asked if I knew the purpose of his investigation. I replied, "No." He said it was concerning a complaint about my assignment of an overweight female commander to the DFA job in the naval hospital at Pensacola, Florida. I was not surprised that someone had complained, but I also was not concerned, because I was comfortable that I had followed all the proper procedures for this assignment.

His first comment made me a little weary because he informed me that the complaint was because I had succumbed to the pressure of at least one RADM and he believed that two RADMs had pushed me for this assignment. He held up a sheet of paper that he said he had retrieved from my files as the detailer and asked me if the initials on the paper were mine. I was too far removed to see the paper but indicated that if he retrieved them from my files it was more than likely that they were my initials. I asked what the paper was. He said that it was a reply from the Deputy Surgeon General, who at the time of the assignment was the Chief of the Medical Service Corps, regarding assignments that I had made that month. I said that this was routine and that unless he had a question about an assignment I would normally initial the email and file it. I asked if he had asked any questions in the email. He said, "No." I listened to his further comments building his case and then he asked me for comments. I asked him if he had checked with the weight control personnel at BuPers about this assignment and he said that he had and they indicated that they had provided me guidance and had approved the assignment. I then asked him, "So what is the issue?" He said the issue was not whether I had or had not dotted all my I's and crossed all of my T's, but whether or not I was influenced in my decisions by one or both of the rear admirals. I said, "Absolutely not." He asked if either the current Deputy Chief of BuMed or the current Chief of the Medical Service Corps had discussed this assignment with me. I told him that of course I had mentioned the assignment during my weekly meeting with the then Chief of the Corps, the current Deputy BuMed, but that he had no comment. I did not know if he was comfortable with the assignment or not because he did not comment on it.

Then the discussion got ugly. The Navy IG smiled and said, "Come on, Captain. I have been around the Navy long enough to know that if an admiral wants something a captain is not going to argue with him about it. You know he influenced this assignment."

I asked the IG if he was calling me a liar. He said, "Call it what you want. You will not convince me that you were not influenced."

I stood up and told the IG that as far as I was concerned he came to see me with preconceived notions that I would not be honest and that this interview was over. If he wanted to talk to me again it would be with my lawyer present.

I was not back in my work area five minutes when the CinC's IG was at my desk. He said, "Hugh, you have got to return to the interview." I said, "I am not talking to that ass anymore. He came down here with his mind made up and nothing I say is going to make a difference." He said that he would have to brief the CinC's Chief of Staff on this matter and that I probably had not heard the last of this issue. I informed the CinC's IG that I had agreed to talk to the "ass" but only if a lawyer of my choosing were present.

I never heard from the Navy's IG again, but he was not through. His findings were that I had been influenced by the two admirals and his recommendation was that the Deputy Surgeon General have a letter of censure placed in his record and that the second star promotion that the current Chief of the Medical Service Corps had recommended be rescinded.

I was tempted to make an issue out of this decision by the Navy but decided that nothing I had to say was going to change what had occurred.

****

My current surgeon's rotation date arrived and though this was a nominative billet (one where each service is requested to provide a candidate) it had always been filled by the Air Force. Well, the Deputy

CinC had an Army colonel that he wanted in the job and though nomination request went out to all three services the Army got the job. I hated to see my current surgeon depart; he was one hell of a boss.

The new CinC Surgeon arrived and immediately we saw the changes in the way we were doing business. There was a lieutenant colonel Army physician and an lieutenant colonel Army physician's assistant on the staff. Colonel Hall had allowed these two officers to travel with the CinC when he was going wherever. The new Army colonel made it clear that only he would be traveling with the CinC.

I was not immune to this new surgeon. When I briefed him on what I had been doing in the Middle East he seemed stunned. He asked me when was my next trip and what was the issue. I told him that I had a trip planned to Kuwait to present what I hoped would be the final draft of an agreement to preposition an Army field hospital in Kuwait. I told him that Dr. Mohamsa and I had been working on this for almost two years. I informed him that Dr. Mohamsa had agreed with the wording of the agreement and that the CinC legal staff had also approved the agreement.

My next trip was for me to accompany Dr. Mohamsa to visit with the crown prince responsible for the Kuwaiti military. He would give the final approval. Dr. Mohamsa had assured me that he had already discussed the agreement with the crown prince and that he would approve the agreement. My new boss informed me that he would be going with me on this trip.

Well, I got his true mantel when we got to Kuwait and we were invited to the senior medical officer of the Army medical facility's going away dinner. The doctor chose to not do anything fancy. He wanted to visit his favorite shawarma stand and have several sandwiches and a glass of pomegranate juice. It was after normal business hours so we sat on the front steps of a bank near the shawarma stand and ate our dinner. Later when we were alone, the colonel lit into me. He said he was embarrassed that I would allow the doctor to treat him, the CinC's Surgeon, this way. I was shocked. I told him that it was the doctor's going away and it was his choice. He invited us, but we did not have to attend. I could tell he was not happy with my comment.

The next day we met with the U.S. embassy person that was to accompany us and Dr. Mohamsa to the meeting with the crown prince. During this meeting the CinC's Surgeon informed the embassy person that he would be going with him, but I would not. I could not believe what I was hearing. After me working on this for over two years he cuts me out of the final act! I went back to the hotel and started to pack my bags.

When the surgeon returned to the hotel he was shocked to hear that I had departed Kuwait on my way back to Tampa. He was expecting me to go with him to Qatar and Bahrain.

When he returned to Tampa the first day back at work he called me into his office. He tried to restrain his temper but eventually he let go. He asked me, "Just who do you think you are to go off and leave me without my permission?" I told him that maybe I had misinterpreted his actions in Kuwait but when he dismissed me from the signing of the agreement I figured he did not need my assistance, so I came home.

I took this opportunity to inform him that I had just about finished the current OPlan that was being updated and that I did not see any other planning evolutions in the near future. In addition, I said that since I had nothing to do for the next six months I had gone ahead and submitted my retirement papers.

He said nothing else so I said, "With your permission I will withdraw." He just looked at me and with that, I walked out of his office.

Later his deputy, also an Army colonel, came to me and asked what had happened. I liked and respected the deputy. I told him what had happened and he shook his head. About twenty minutes after he left my cubicle he returned and informed me that the surgeon would like to speak with me. I shrugged my shoulders and said okay. The deputy came with me to the surgeon's office. The surgeon asked me to be seated. He then said that he had not intended to upset me but he just decided that issues on the level that I was dealing with were better handled at his level. I said, "Yes, Sir."

He asked if I were serious about my retirement request. I assured him that our situation had nothing to do with my decision. I told him that at some point he would come to the same decision. I said, "You just know when it is time, and for me the time has come."

I said that I had submitted the request for 1 Feb 2000. He asked me how many years of service I had and when I told him forty I could tell he did not believe me. He asked how I was allowed to serve that long and I explained that my sixteen years of enlisted service did not count against my commissioned service. So, I could serve up to thirty years commissioned service or age sixty-five, whichever came first. I said, "I was an E-9 when I was commissioned." I could see that he was not sure what to say or do with me. After a few minutes I asked him if there was anything further. He just shook his head and I left his office.

The deputy came back to my cubicle and apologized for the surgeon's behavior. I told the Deputy that the CinC Surgeon was the boss and had every right to run his office as he saw fit. The deputy asked me to reconsider my retirement request. I told him that the new surgeon had nothing to do with my decision. I was tired and knew that it was time to call it quits. I had no regrets and I held no animosity towards anyone.

My loving wife Wanda stood by me in every decision I made. She just wanted me to be happy and she knew that another year working for the current surgeon was not going to be easy for me.

TWENTY-NINE

B Y OCTOBER 1999 I HAD COMPLETED THE REVIEW of the OPlan that we had been working on, so my relief would not be stuck with that when he arrived. I requested that I be allowed to use my sixty days leave that I had available and had my retirement ceremony in late October 1999.

The Deputy Surgeon was the master of ceremonies at my retirement. He did something that almost brought me to tears. There was a group of military members lined up next to the stage. Each member represented each of my pay grades that I had held during my military career. There were fifteen total and they were from all branches of the service. He explained later that he could not round up enough Sailors. I told him that with all of my joint duty it was more appropriate to have all services represented.

General Edwards was my guest speaker and he mentioned that I was the only one in the command that was senior to him. Of course he was referring to time in service, not rank. He also spoke of his days in Vietnam as a young Marine Corps officer who was twice wounded, and how at least one of those wounds could have been life threatening but a young, very competent "Doc" Navy hospital corpsman was there to administer the aid needed to save not only his life but his career.

As I sat there listening to the general's remarks my mind wandered to yesteryear. I thought of Juan and all the other young men that had died or been maimed in the Vietnam War. I thought of the warehouse with the numerous missing footlockers. I thought of the young Vietnamese that I had killed while trying to save him. And of course I thought of Short Round and wondered if he survived the war and if so what he was doing. I realized for the first time that as bad as it was the Vietnam War was my defining moment. That was the time that I grew up and became a man. It was the period of my life that set me on the road to future successes.

General Edwards presented me the Defense Superior Service Medal upon my retirement. In total I had twenty-seven medals and service awards but, most importantly, I had a lifetime of memories to share in my retirement.

After a career that expanded advancement from the lowest enlisted rating to the highest enlisted rating, and being commissioned and advancing from ensign to captain, I am completely comfortable with my accomplishments and know that I was only able to reach these accomplishments because of the experiences I had and the love and support of Wanda.

All of the things I have discussed in this story made me think of all of the choices that I had made during my forty year career. While many of the choices were ones that I alone had to make, I always gave Wanda her opportunity to provide her input. She saved me more than once from doing something that might have caused our lives to turn out differently. I made some bad choices, but more good ones than bad. As a result of many choices that at the time I did not even recognize as choices, Wanda and I are now living the good life. We travel, I fish at every opportunity and I have read more books since retirement than I had read in my entire life. Wanda and I exercise daily and are active in our local senior center. We do not miss the Navy, but we miss the people and the excitement of where were we going to live next. But, we are enjoying the freedom of doing what we want, when we want.

And to think it all started with an uneducated kid from a cotton mill village who was provided the opportunities to become whatever he set his goals to be. Thank you, Navy!

Life truly is about choices.

About the Author

HUGH C. SULLIVAN, JR., CAPTAIN, UNITED STATES NAVY (RET) was born in Columbia, South Carolina, on 4 November 1942. His military service began in February 1961 when he enlisted in the South Carolina National Guard. His active naval service began in June 1961 and he served sixteen years enlisted service. Hugh is a graduate of George Washington University where he received a BS degree in Hospital Administration, Pepperdine University where he received a Master of Arts Degree in Human Resources Management, and the Armed Forces Staff College.

His awards include twenty-two Campaigns and Service Ribbons and Medals, and the Defense Superior Service Medal, Meritorious Service Medal (with four Gold Stars), Navy & Marine Corps Commendation Medal, Joint Service Achievement Medal, Navy & Marine Corps Achievement Medal, Enlisted Good Conduct Medal (with three Gold Stars) and the Combat Action Ribbon. Captain Sullivan was the 1998 recipient of AMSCON (Association of Medical Service Corps Officers of the Navy) Captain Clarence Gibbs Navy Annual Leadership Award. He was the first Plans, Operations and Medical Intelligence Officer (POMI) to receive this award.

Hugh is married to the former Wanda Perdue. They have three daughters and three grandsons, and currently reside in Tampa, Florida.

CPSIA information can be obtained
at www.ICGtesting.com
Printed in the USA
LVOW04s0907210516

489316LV00008B/55/P